HERO TALES

JAMES BALDWIN

1st WORLD
LIBRARY
Literary Society

Hero Tales

James Baldwin

© 1st World Library, 2006
PO Box 2211
Fairfield, IA 52556
www.1stworldlibrary.com
First Edition

LCCN: 2006907717

Softcover ISBN: 1-4218-2431-0
Hardcover ISBN: 1-4218-2331-4
eBook ISBN: 1-4218-2531-7

Purchase *"Hero Tales"*
as a traditional bound book at:
www.1stWorldLibrary.com/purchase.asp?ISBN=1-4218-2431-0

1st World Library is a literary, educational organization
dedicated to:

- Creating a free internet library of downloadable ebooks

- Hosting writing competitions and offering book
publishing scholarships.

Interested in more 1st World Library books?
contact: literacy@1stworldlibrary.com
Check us out at: www.1stworldlibrary.com

1st World Library Literary Society

Giving Back to the World

"If you want to work on the core problem, it's early school literacy."

- James Barksdale, former CEO of Netscape

"No skill is more crucial to the future of a child, or to a democratic and prosperous society, than literacy."

- Los Angeles Times

Literacy... means far more than learning how to read and write... The aim is to transmit... knowledge and promote social participation."

- UNESCO

"Literacy is not a luxury, it is a right and a responsibility. If our world is to meet the challenges of the twenty-first century we must harness the energy and creativity of all our citizens."

- President Bill Clinton

"Parents should be encouraged to read to their children, and teachers should be equipped with all available techniques for teaching literacy, so the varying needs and capacities of individual kids can be taken into account."

- Hugh Mackay

TO

CARRIE EDITH AND NELLIE MAY

INTRODUCTION

In the world's literature there are certain stories which, told ages ago, can never be forgotten. They have within them that which gives pleasure to all intelligent men, women and children. They appeal to the sympathies, the desires, and the admiration of all sorts and conditions of mankind. These are the stories that are said to be immortal. They have been repeated and re-repeated in many forms and to all kinds of audiences. They have been recited and sung in royal palaces, in the halls of mediaeval castles, and by the camp fires of warring heroes. Parents have taught them to their children, and generation after generation has preserved their memory. They have been written on parchment and printed in books, translated into many languages, abridged, extended, edited, and "adapted." But through all these changes and the vicissitudes of time, they still preserve the qualities that have made them so universally popular.

Chief among these masterpieces of imagination are the tales of gods and heroes that have come down to us from the golden age of Greece, and particularly the tales of Troy that cluster around the narratives of old Homer in his "Iliad" and "Odyssey." Three thousand years or more have passed since they were first recited, and yet they have lost none of their original charm. Few persons of intelligence are unacquainted with these tales, for our literature abounds in allusions to them; and no one who pretends to the possession of culture or learning can afford to be ignorant of them.

Second only in interest, especially to us of Anglo-Saxon descent, are the hero tales of the ancient North and the stirring legends connected with the "Nibelungen Lied." Of much later origin than the Greek stories, and somewhat inferior to them in refinement of thought and delicacy of imagery, these tales partake of the rugged, forceful character of the people among whom they were composed. Yet, with all their austerity and sternness, they are replete with vivid action, and they charm us by their very strength and the lessons which they teach of heroic endurance and the triumph of eternal justice.

Scarcely inferior to these latter, but not so well known to English-speaking people, are the tales of knighthood and chivalry that commemorate the romantic deeds of Charlemagne and his paladins. Written in various languages, and at periods widely separated, these tales present a curious mixture of fact and fiction, of the real and the marvellous, of the beautiful and the grotesque, of pagan superstition and Christian devotion. Although there were, in truth, no knights in the time of Charlemagne, and the institution of chivalry did not exist until many years later, yet these legends are of value as portraying life and manners in that period of history which we call the Dark Ages; and their pictures of knightly courage and generosity, faithfulness, and loyalty, appeal to our nobler feelings and stir our hearts with admiration.

To know something of these three great cycles, or groups, of classic and romantic stories - the hero tales of Troy, those of the ancient North, and those of Charlemagne - is essential to the acquirement of refined literary tastes. For this knowledge will go far toward helping its possessor to enjoy many things in our modern literature that would otherwise be puzzling or obscure. The importance, therefore, of placing some of the best of such tales early within the reach of school children and all young readers cannot be disputed.

In three volumes somewhat larger than the present one - "A Story of the Golden Age," "The Story of Siegfried," and "The Story of Roland" - I have already endeavored to introduce young readers to the most interesting portions of these great cycles of romance, narrating in each the adventures of the hero who is the central figure in the group of legends or tales under consideration. The present volume, made up of selections from these earlier books, has been prepared in response to repeated suggestions that certain portions of them, and especially some of the independent shorter stories, are well adapted to use in reading-classes at school. Of the seventeen stories herein presented, nine are from the "Golden Age," four from "Siegfried," and four from "Roland." They are, for the most part, episodes, complete in themselves, and connected only by a slender thread with the main narrative. Their intrinsic value is in no way diminished by being thus separated from their former setting, and each tale being independent of the others, they lend themselves more readily to the demands of the schoolroom.

It is well to observe that in no case have I endeavored to repeat the story in its exact original form. To have done so would have defeated the purpose in view; for without proper adaptation such stories are usually neither interesting nor intelligible to children. I have therefore recast and rearranged, using my own words, and adding here a touch of color and here a fanciful idea, as the narrative has seemed to permit or as my audience of school children may demand. Nevertheless, in the end, the essential features of each tale - those which give it value in its original form - remain unchanged.

CONTENTS

HOW APOLLO CAME TO PARNASSUS

A very long time ago, Apollo was born in the island of Delos. When the glad news of his birth was told, Earth smiled, and decked herself with flowers; the nymphs of Delos sang songs of joy that were heard to the utmost bounds of Greece; and choirs of white swans flew seven times around the island, piping notes of praise to the pure being who had come to dwell among men. Then Zeus looked down from high Olympus, and crowned the babe with a golden head-band, and put into his hands a silver bow and a sweet-toned lyre such as no man had ever seen; and he gave him a team of white swans to drive, and bade him go forth to teach men the things which are right and good, and to make light that which is hidden in darkness.

So Apollo arose, beautiful as the morning sun, and journeyed through many lands, seeking a dwelling place. He stopped for a time at the foot of Mount Olympus, and played so sweetly upon his lyre that Zeus and all his court were entranced. Then he wandered up and down through the whole length of the Thessalian land; but nowhere could he find a spot in which he was willing to dwell. At length he climbed into his car, and bade his swan team fly with him to the country of the Hyperboreans beyond the far-off northern mountains. Forth-with they obeyed; and through the pure regions of the upper air they bore him, winging their way ever northward. They carried him over many an unknown land, and on the seventh day they came to the Snowy Mountains where the griffins, with   lion bodies and eagle wings, guard the golden treasures of the North.

In these mountains, the North Wind has his home; and from his deep caves he now and then comes forth, chilling with his cold and angry breath the orchards and the fair fields of Greece, and bringing death and dire disasters In his train. But northward this blustering Boreas cannot blow, for the heaven-towering mountains stand like a wall against him, and drive him back. Hence it is that beyond these mountains the storms of winter never come, but one happy springtime runs through all the year. There the flowers bloom, and the grain ripens, and the fruits drop mellowing to the earth, and the red wine is pressed from the luscious grape, every day the same.

The Hyperboreans who dwell in that favored land know neither pain nor sickness, nor wearying labor nor eating care; but their youth is as unfading as the springtime, and old age with its wrinkles and its sorrows is evermore a stranger to them. The spirit of evil, which would lead all men to err, has never found entrance among them, and they are free from vile passions and unworthy thoughts; and among them there is neither war, nor wicked deeds, nor fear of the avenging Furies, for their hearts are pure and clean, and never burdened with the love of self.

When the swan team of silver-bowed Apollo had carried him over the Snowy Mountains, they alighted in the Hyperborean land. And the people welcomed Apollo with shouts of joy and songs of triumph, as one for whom they had long been waiting. He took up his abode there, and dwelt with them one whole year, delighting them with his presence, and ruling over them as their king. But when twelve moons had passed, he bethought him that the toiling, suffering men of Greece needed most his aid and care. Therefore he bade the Hyperboreans farewell, and again went up into his sun-bright car; and his winged team carried him back to the land of his birth.

Long time Apollo sought a place where he might build a temple to which men might come to learn of him and to seek his help in time of need. At length he came to a broad plain, by the shore of a beautiful lake; and there he began to build a house, for the land was a pleasant one, well-watered, and rich in grain and fruit. But the nymph that lived in the lake liked not to have Apollo so near her, lest men seeing and loving him should forget to honor her; and one day, garmented with mosses and crowned with lilies, she came and stood before him in the sunlight.

"Apollo of the silver bow," said she, "have you not made a mistake in choosing this place for a dwelling? These rich plains around us will not always be as peaceful as now; for their very richness will tempt the spoiler, and the song of the cicada will then give place to the din of battle. Even in times of peace you would hardly have a quiet hour here: for great herds of cattle come crowding down every day to my lake for water; the noisy ploughman, driving his team afield, disturbs the morning hour with his boorish shouts; and boys and dogs keep up a constant din, and make life in this place a burden."

"Fair nymph," said Apollo, "I had hoped to dwell here in thy happy vale, a neighbor and friend to thee. Yet, since this place is not what it seems to be, whither shall I go, and where shall I build my house?"

"Go to the cleft in Mount Parnassus," answered the nymph. "There thou canst dwell in peace, and men will come from all parts of the world to do thee honor."

And so Apollo went down to Parnassus, and there in the cleft of the mountain he laid the foundations of his shrine.

Then he called the master architects of the world, Trophonius and Agamedes, and gave to them the building of the high walls and the massive roof. When they had finished their work, he said, "Say now what reward you most desire for your labor, and I will give it you."

"Give us," said the brothers, "that which is the best for men."

"It is well," answered Apollo. "When the full moon is seen above the mountain-tops, you shall have your wish."

But when the moon rose full and clear above the heights, the two brothers were dead.

Apollo was pleased with the place which he had chosen for a home; for there he found rest and quiet, and neither the hum of labor nor the din of battle was likely ever to enter. One thing, however, must needs be done before he could have perfect peace. There lived near the foot of the mountain a huge serpent called Python, which was the terror of all the land. Oftentimes, coming out of its den, this monster attacked the flocks and herds, and sometimes even their keepers; and it had been known to carry little children and helpless women to its den, and there devour them.

The men of the place came to Apollo, and prayed him to drive out or destroy their terrible enemy. So, taking in hand his silver bow, he sallied out at break of day to meet the monster when it should issue from its slimy cave. The vile creature shrank back when it saw its radiant enemy, and would fain have hidden itself in the deep gorges of the mountain. But Apollo quickly launched a swift arrow at it, crying, "Thou bane of man, lie thou upon the earth, and enrich it with thy dead body!" The never-erring arrow sped to the mark; and the great beast died, wallowing in its gore. And the people in their joy came out to meet the archer, singing paeans in his praise. They crowned him with wild flowers and wreaths of olives, and hailed him as the Pythian king; and the nightingales sang to him in the groves, and the swallows and cicadas twittered and tuned their melodies in harmony with his lyre.

But as yet there were no priests in Apollo's temple; and he pondered, long doubting, as to whom he should choose. One day he stood upon the mountain's topmost peak, whence he could view all Greece and the seas around it. Far away in the south, he spied a little ship sailing from Crete to sandy Pylos; and the men who were on board were Cretan merchants.

"These men shall serve in my temple!" he cried.

Upward he sprang, and high he soared above the sea; then swiftly descending like a fiery star, he plunged into the waves. There he changed himself into the form of a dolphin, and swam with speed to overtake the vessel.

Long before the ship had reached Pylos, the mighty fish came up with it, and struck its stern. The crew were dumb with terror, and sat still in their places; their oars were motionless; the sail hung limp and useless from the mast. Yet the vessel sped through the waves with the speed of the wind, for the dolphin was driving it forward by the force of his fins. Past many a headland, past Pylos and other pleasant harbors, they hastened. Vainly did the pilot try to land at each favorable place: the ship would not obey her helm. They rounded the headland of Araxus, and came into the long bay of Crissa; and there the dolphin left off guiding the vessel, and swam playfully around it, while a brisk west wind filled the sail, and bore the voyagers safely into port.

Then the dolphin changed into the form of a glowing star, which, shooting high into the heavens, lit up the whole world with its glory; and as the awe-stricken crew stood gazing at the wonder, it fell with the quickness of light upon Mount Parnassus. Into his temple Apollo hastened, and there he kindled an undying fire. Then, in the form of a handsome youth, with golden hair falling in waves upon his shoulders, he hastened to the beach to welcome the Cretan strangers.

"Hall, seamen!" he cried. "Who are you, and whence do you come? Shall I greet you as friends and guests, or shall I know you as robbers bringing death and distress to many a fair home?"

Then answered the Cretan captain, "Fair stranger, the gods have brought us hither; for by no wish of our own have we come. We are Cretan merchants, and we were on our way to Pylos with stores of merchandise, to barter with the tradesmen of that city. But some unknown being, whose might is greater than the might of men, has carried us far beyond our wished-for port, even to this unknown shore. Tell us now, we pray thee, what land is this? And who art thou who lookest so like a god?"

"Friends and guests, for such indeed you must be," answered the radiant youth, "think never again of sailing upon the wine-faced sea, but draw now your vessel high up on the beach. And when you have brought out all your goods and built an altar upon the shore, take of your white barley which you have with you, and offer it reverently to Phoebus Apollo. For I am he; and it was I who brought you hither, so that you might keep my temple, and make known my wishes unto men. And since it was in the form of a dolphin that you first saw me, let the town which stands around my temple be known as Delphi [Dolphin], and let men worship me there as Apollo Delphinius."

James Baldwin

Then the Cretans did as he had bidden them: they drew their vessel high up on the white beach, and when they had unladen it of their goods, they built an altar on the shore, and offered white barley to Phoebus Apollo, and gave thanks to the ever-living powers who had saved them from the terrors of the deep. After they had feasted and rested from their long voyage, they turned their faces toward Parnassus; and Apollo, playing sweeter music than men had ever heard, led the way; and the folk of Delphi, with choirs of boys and maidens, came to meet them, singing songs of victory as they helped the Cretans up the steep pathway to the temple in the cleft of the mountain.

"I leave you now to have sole care of my temple," said Apollo. "I charge you to keep it well. Deal righteously with all men; let no unclean thing pass your lips; forget self; guard well your thoughts, and keep your hearts free from guile. If you do these things, you shall be blessed with length of days and all that makes life glad. But if you forget my words, and deal treacherously with men, and cause any to wander from the path of right, then shall you be driven forth homeless and accursed, and others shall take your places in the service of my house."

Then the bright youth left them and hastened away to Mount Olympus. But every year he came again, and looked into his house, and spoke words of warning and of hope to his servants; and men say that he has often been seen on Parnassus, playing his lyre to the listening Muses, or with his sister, Artemis, chasing the mountain deer.

THE HUNT IN THE WOOD OF CALYDON

RELATED BY AUTOLYCUS[1]

"When I was younger than I am to-day," said the old chief, as they sat one evening in the light of the blazing brands - "when I was much younger than now, it was my fortune to take part in the most famous boar hunt the world has ever known.

"There lived at that time, in Calydon, a mighty chief named Oineus - and, indeed, I know not but that he still lives. Oineus was rich in vineyards and in orchards, and no other man in all Greece was happier or more blessed than he. He had married, early in life, the Princess Althea, fairest of the maidens of Acarnania; and to them a son had been born, golden-haired and beautiful, whom they called Meleager.

"When Meleager was yet but one day old, his father held him in his arms, and prayed to Zeus and the mighty powers above: 'Grant, Father Zeus, and all ye deathless ones, that this my son may be the foremost among the men of Greece. And let it come to pass, that when they see his valiant deeds, his country-men shall say, "Behold, this youth is greater than his father," and all of one accord shall hail him as their guardian king.'

"Then his mother, Althea, weeping tears of joy, prayed that the boy might grow up to be pure-minded and gentle,

James Baldwin

the hope and pride of his parents, and the delight and staff of their declining years.

"Scarcely had the words of prayer died from her lips, when there came into her chamber the three unerring Fates who spin the destinies of men. White-robed and garlanded, they stood beside the babe, and with unwearied fingers drew out the lines of his untried life. Clotho held the golden distaff in her hand, and twirled and twisted the delicate thread. Lachesis, now sad, now hopeful, with her long white fingers held the hour-glass, and framed her lips to say, 'It is enough.' And Atropos, blind and unpitying as the future always is, stood ready, with cruel shears, to clip the twist in twain. Busily and silently Clotho spun; and the golden thread, thin as a spider's web, yet beautiful as a sunbeam, grew longer and more golden between her skilful fingers. Then Lachesis cried out, 'It is finished!' But Atropos hid her shears beneath her mantle, and said, 'Not so. Behold, there is a brand burning upon the hearth. Wait until it is all burned into ashes and smoke, and then I will cut the thread of the child's life. Spin on, sweet Clotho!'

"Quick as thought, Althea sprang forward, snatched the blazing brand from the hearth, and quenched its flame in a jar of water; and when she knew that not a single spark was left glowing upon it, she locked it safely in a chest where none but she could find it. As she did this, the pitiless sisters vanished from her sight, saying as they flitted through the air, 'We bide our time.'

"Meleager grew up to be a tall and fair and gentle youth; and when at last he became a man, he sailed on the ship Argo, with Jason and the great heroes of that day, in search of the Golden Fleece. Many brave deeds were his in foreign lands; and when he came home again to Calydon, he brought with him a fair young wife, gentle

Cleopatra, daughter of Idas the boaster.

"Oineus had gathered in his harvest; and he was glad and thankful in his heart, because his fields had yielded plenteously; his vines had been loaded with purple grapes, and his orchards filled with abundance of pleasant fruit. Grateful, as men should always be, to the givers of peace and plenty, he held within his halls a harvest festival, to which he invited the brave and beautiful of all the country round. Happy was this feast, and the hours were bright with smiles and sunshine; and men forgot sorrow and labor, and thought only of the gladness of life.

"Then Oineus took of the first-fruits of his fields and his vineyards and his orchards, and offered them with much thankfulness to the givers of good. But he forgot to deck the shrine of Artemis with gifts, little thinking that the huntress queen cared for anything which mortal men might offer her. Ah, woful mistake was that! For, in her anger at the slight, Artemis sent a savage boar, with ivory tusks and foaming mouth, to overrun the lands of Calydon. Many a field did the monster ravage, many a tree uproot; and all the growing vines, which late had borne so rich a vintage, were trampled to the ground.

"Sadly troubled was Oineus, and he knew not what to do. For the fierce beast could not be slain, but with his terrible tusks he had sent many a rash hunter to an untimely death. Then the young man Meleager said, 'I will call together the heroes of Greece, and we will hunt the boar in the wood of Calydon.'

"So at the call of Meleager, the warriors flocked from every land, to join in the hunt of the fierce wild boar. Among them came Castor and Pollux, the twin brothers; and Idas, the boaster, the father-in-law of Meleager; and mighty Jason, captain of the Argo; and Atalanta, the swift-footed daughter of Iasus, of Arcadia; and many Acarnanian huntsmen led by the brothers of Queen Althea. Thither also did I hasten, although men spitefully said that I was far more skilful in taking tame beasts than in slaying wild ones.

"Nine days we feasted in the halls of Oineus; and every day we tried our skill with bows and arrows, and tested the strength of our well-seasoned spears. On the tenth, the bugles sounded, and hounds and huntsmen gathered in the courtyard of the chief, chafing for the hunt.

"Soon we sallied forth from the town, a hundred huntsmen, with dogs innumerable. Through the fields and orchards, laid waste by the savage beast, we passed; and Atalanta, keen of sight and swift of foot, her long hair floating in the wind behind her, led all the rest. It was not long until, in a narrow dell once green with vines and trees, but now strewn thick with withered branches, we roused the fierce creature from his lair.

"At first he fled, followed closely by the baying hounds. Then suddenly he faced his foes; with gnashing teeth and bloodshot eyes, he charged furiously upon them. A score of hounds were slain outright; and Cepheus, of Arcadia, rushing blindly onward, was caught by the beast, and torn in pieces by his sharp tusks. Then swift-footed Atalanta, bounding forward, struck the beast a deadly blow with her spear. He stopped short, and ceased his furious onslaught.

"Terrible were the cries of the wounded creature, as he made a last charge upon the huntsmen. But Meleager with a skilful sword-thrust pierced his heart and the beast fell weltering in his gore. Great joy filled the hearts of the Calydonians when they saw the scourge of their land laid low and helpless. They quickly flayed the beast, and the heroes who had shared in the hunt divided the flesh among them; but the head and the bristly hide they offered to Meleager.

"'Not to me does the prize belong,' he cried, 'but to Atalanta, the swift-footed huntress. For the first wound - the true death stroke, indeed - was given by her; and to her, woman though she be, all honor and the prize must be awarded.'

"With these words, he bore the grinning head and the bristly hide to the young huntress, and laid them at her feet. Then his uncles, the brothers of Queen Althea, rushed angrily forward, saying that no woman should ever bear a prize away from them; and they seized the hide, and would have taken it away, had not Meleager forbidden them. Yet they would not loose their hold upon the prize, but drew their swords, and wrathfully threatened Meleager's life.

"The hero's heart grew hot within him, and he shrank not from the affray. Long and fearful was the struggle - uncles against nephew; but in the end the brothers of Althea lay bleeding upon the ground, while the victor brought again the boar's hide, and laid it the second time at Atalanta's feet. The fair huntress took the prize, and carried it away with her to deck her father's hall in the pleasant Arcadian land. And the heroes, when they had feasted nine other days with King Oineus, betook themselves to their own homes.

"But the hearts of the Acarnanian hunters were bitter toward Meleager, because no part of the wild boar was awarded to them. They called their chiefs around them, and all their brave men, and made war upon King Oineus and Meleager. Many battles did they fight round Calydon; yet so long as Meleager led his warriors to the fray, the Acarnanians fared but ill.

"Then Queen Althea, filled with grief for her brothers' untimely fate, forgot her love for her son, and prayed that her Acarnanian kinsmen might prevail against him. Upon the hard earth she knelt: she beat the ground with her hands, and heaped the dust about her; and, weeping bitter tears, she called upon Hades to avenge her of Meleager. And even as she prayed, the pitiless Furies, wandering amid the darkness, heard her cries, and came, obedient to her wishes.

"When Meleager heard that his mother had turned against him, he withdrew in sorrow to his own house, and sought comfort and peace with his wife, fair Cleopatra; and he would not lead his warriors any more to battle against the Acarnanians. Then the enemy besieged the city: a fearful tumult rose about the gates; the high towers were assaulted, and everywhere the Calydonians were driven back dismayed and beaten.

"With uplifted hands and tearful eyes, King Oineus and the elders of the city came to Meleager, and besought him to take the field again. Rich gifts they offered him. They bade him choose for his own the most fertile farm in Calydon - at the least fifty acres, half for tillage and half for vines; but he would not listen to them.

"The din of battle thickened outside the gates; the towers shook with the thundering blows of the besiegers. Old Oineus with trembling limbs climbed up the stairway to his son's secluded chamber, and, weeping, prayed him to come down and save the city from fire and pillage. Still he kept silent, and went not. His sisters came, and his most trusted friends. 'Come, Meleager,' they prayed, 'forget thy grief, and think only of our great need. Aid thy people, or we shall all perish!'

"None of these prayers moved him. The gates were beaten

down; the enemy was within the walls; the tide of battle shook the very tower where Meleager sat; the doom of Calydon seemed to be sealed. Then came the fair Cleopatra, and knelt before her husband, and besought him to withhold no longer the aid which he alone could give. 'O Meleager,' she sobbed, 'none but thou can save us. Wilt thou sit still, and see the city laid in ashes, thy dearest friends slaughtered, and thy wife and sweet babes dragged from their homes and sold into cruel slavery?'

"Then Meleager rose and girded on his armor. To the streets he hastened, shouting his well-known battle cry. Eagerly and hopefully did the Calydonian warriors rally around him. Fiercely did they meet the foe. Terrible was the bloodshed. Back from the battered gates and the crumbling wall the Acarnanian hosts were driven. A panic seized upon them. They turned and fled, and not many of them escaped the swords of Meleager's men.

"Again there was peace in Calydon, and the orchards of King Oineus blossomed and bore fruit as of old; but the gifts and large rewards which the elders had promised to Meleager were forgotten. He had saved his country, but his countrymen were ungrateful.

"Meleager again laid aside his war gear, and sought the quiet of his own home and the cheering presence of fair Cleopatra. For the remembrance of his mother's curse and his country's ingratitude weighed heavily on his mind, and he cared no longer to mingle with his fellow men.

"Then it was that Althea's hatred of her son waxed stronger, and she thought of the half-burned brand which she had hidden, and of the words which the Fatal Sisters had spoken so many years before.

"'He is no longer my son,' said she, 'and why should I

James Baldwin

withhold the burning of the brand? He can never again bring comfort to my heart; for the blood of my brothers, whom I loved, is upon his head.'

"And she took the charred billet from the place where she had hidden it, and cast it again into the flames. And as it slowly burned away, so did the life of Meleager wane. Lovingly he bade his wife farewell; softly he whispered a prayer to the unseen powers above; and as the flickering flames of the fatal brand died into darkness, he gently breathed his last.

"Then sharp-toothed remorse seized upon Althea, and the mother love which had slept in her bosom was reawakened. Too late, also, the folk of Calydon remembered who it was that had saved them from slavery and death. Down into the comfortless halls of Hades, Althea hastened to seek her son's forgiveness. The loving heart of Cleopatra, surcharged with grief, was broken; and her gentle spirit fled to the world of shades to meet that of her hero-husband. Meleager's sisters would not be consoled, so great was the sorrow which had come upon them; and they wept and lamented day and night, until kind Artemis in pity for their youth changed them into the birds which we call Meleagrides."

[1]Autolycus was a famous mountain chief who lived in rude state on the slopes of Parnassus and was noted for his courage and cunning. He was the grandfather of Odysseus (Ulysses), to whom the story is supposed to have been related.

THE CHOICE OF HERCULES

When Hercules was a fair-faced youth, and life was all before him, he went out one morning to do an errand for his stepfather. But as he walked his heart was full of bitter thoughts; and he murmured because others no better than himself were living in ease and pleasure, while for him there was naught but a life of labor and pain.

As he thought upon these things, he came to a place where two roads met; and he stopped, not certain which one to take.

The road on his right was hilly and rough; there was no beauty in it or about it: but he saw that it led straight toward the blue mountains in the far distance.

The road on his left was broad and smooth, with shade trees on either side, where sang an innumerable choir of birds; and it went winding among green meadows, where bloomed countless flowers: but it ended in fog and mist long before it reached the wonderful blue mountains in the distance.

While the lad stood in doubt as to these roads, he saw two fair women coming toward him, each on a different road. The one who came by the flowery way reached him first, and Hercules saw that she was as beautiful as a summer day.

James Baldwin

Her cheeks were red, her eyes sparkled; she, spoke warm, persuasive words. "O noble youth," she said, "be no longer bowed down with labor and sore trials, but come and follow me, I will lead you into pleasant paths, where there are no storms to disturb and no troubles to annoy. You shall live in ease, with one unending round of music and mirth; and you shall not want for anything that makes life joyous - sparkling wine, or soft couches, or rich robes, or the loving eyes of beautiful maidens. Come with me, and life shall be to you a day-dream of gladness."

By this time the other fair woman had drawn near, and she now spoke to the lad. "I have nothing to promise you," said she, "save that which you shall win with your own strength. The road upon which I would lead you is uneven and hard, and climbs many a hill, and descends into many a valley and quagmire. The views which you will sometimes get from the hilltops are grand and glorious, but the deep valleys are dark, and the ascent from them is toilsome. Nevertheless, the road leads to the blue mountains of endless fame, which you see far away on the horizon. They cannot be reached without labor; in fact, there is nothing worth having that must not be won by toil. If you would have fruits and flowers, you must plant them and care for them; if you would gain the love of your fellow men, you must love them and suffer for them; if you would enjoy the favor of Heaven, you must make yourself worthy of that favor; if you would have eternal fame, you must not scorn the hard road that leads to it."

Then Hercules saw that this lady, although she was as beautiful as the other, had a countenance pure and gentle, like the sky on a balmy morning in May.

"What is your name?" he asked.

"Some call me Labor," she answered, "but others know me as Virtue."

Then he turned to the first lady. "And what is your name?" he asked.

"Some call me Pleasure," she said, with a bewitching smile,
"but I choose to be known as the Joyous and Happy One."

"Virtue," said Hercules, "I will take thee as my guide! The road of labor and honest effort shall be mine, and my heart shall no longer cherish bitterness or discontent."

And he put his hand into that of Virtue, and entered with her upon the straight and forbidding road which leads to the fair blue mountains on the pale and distant horizon.

ALPHEUS AND ARETHUSA

In Arcadia there is a little mountain stream called Alpheus. It flows through woods and meadows and among the hills for many miles, and then it sinks beneath the rocks. Farther down the valley it rises again, and dancing and sparkling, as if in happy chase of something, it hurries onward towards the plain; but soon it hides itself a second time in underground caverns, making its way through rocky tunnels where the light of day has never been. Then at last it gushes once more from its prison chambers; and, flowing thence with many windings through the fields of Elis, it empties its waters into the sea.

Years ago there was no river Alpheus; the channel through which it flows had not then been hollowed out, and rank grass and tall bending reeds grew thick where now its waters sparkle brightest. It was then that a huntsman, bearing the name of Alpheus, ranged through the woods, and chased the wild deer among the glades and glens of sweet Arcadia. Far away by the lonely sea dwelt his fair young wife, and his lovely babe Orsilochus; but dearer than home or wife or babe to Alpheus, was the free life of the huntsman among the mountain solitudes. For he loved the woods and the blue sky and the singing birds, and the frail flowers upon the hillside; and he longed to live among them always, where his ears could listen to their music, and his eyes look upon their beauty.

"O Artemis, huntress queen!" he cried, "I ask but one boon of thee. Let me ramble forever among these happy scenes!"

Artemis heard him, and answered his prayer. For, as he spoke, a bright vision passed before him. A sweet-faced maiden went tripping down the valley, culling the choicest flowers, and singing of hope and joy and the blessedness of a life pure and true. It was Arethusa, the Arcadian nymph, by some supposed to be a daughter of old Nereus, the elder of the sea.

Then Alpheus heard no more the songs of the birds, or the music of the breeze; he saw no longer the blue sky above him, or the nodding flowers at his feet: he was blind and deaf to all the world, save only the beautiful nymph. Arethusa was the world to him.

He reached out his arms to catch her; but, swifter than a frightened deer, she fled down the valley, through deep ravines and grassy glades and rocky caverns underneath the hills, and out into the grassy meadows, and across the plains of Elis, to the sounding sea. And Alpheus followed, forgetful of everything but the fleeing vision. When, at length, he reached the sea, he looked back; and, lo! he was no longer a huntsman, but a river doomed to meander forever among the scenes, for love of which he had forgotten his wife and his babe and the duties of life. It was thus that Artemis answered his prayer.

And men say that Arethusa, the nymph, was afterwards changed into a fountain; and that to this day, in the far-off island of Ortygia, that fountain gushes from the rocks in an unfailing, crystal stream. But Orsilochus, the babe forgotten by his father, grew to manhood, and in course of time became the king of the seafaring people of Messene.

James Baldwin

THE GOLDEN APPLE

RELATED BY CHEIRON THE CENTAUR[1]

"There is a cavern somewhere on Mount Pelion larger by far and a thousand times more beautiful than this; but its doorway is hidden to mortals, and but few men have ever stood beneath its vaulted roof. In that cavern the ever-living ones who oversee the affairs of men, once held high carnival; for they had met there at the marriage feast of King Peleus, and the woods and rocks of mighty Pelion echoed with the sound of their merry-making. But wherefore should the marriage feast of a mortal be held in such a place and with guests so noble and so great? I will tell you.

"After Peleus had escaped from a plot which some wicked men had made for his destruction, he dwelt long time with me, who am his grandfather. But the days seemed long to him, thus shut out from fellowship with men, and the sun seemed to move slowly in the heavens; and often he would walk around to the other side of the mountain, and sitting upon a great rock, he would gaze for long hours upon the purple waters of the sea. One morning as thus he sat, he saw the sea nymph Thetis come up out of the waves and walk upon the shore beneath him. Fairer than a dream was she - more beautiful than any picture of nymph or goddess. She was clad in a robe of green silk, woven by the sea maidens in their watery grottoes; and there was a chaplet of pearls upon her head, and sandals of sparkling silver were upon her feet.

"As Peleus gazed upon this lovely creature, he heard a voice whispering in his ear. It was the voice of wise Athena.

"'Most luckless of mortal men,' she said, 'there is recompense in store for those who repent of their wrong-doing, and who, leaving the paths of error, turn again to the road of virtue. The immortals have seen thy sorrow for the evil deeds of thy youth, and they have looked with pity upon thee in thy misfortunes. And now thy days of exile and of sore punishment are drawing to an end. Behold the silver-footed Thetis, most beautiful of the nymphs of the sea, whom even the immortals have wooed in vain! She has been sent to this shore, to be won and wedded by thee.'

"Peleus looked up to see the speaker of these words, but he beheld only a blue cloud resting above the mountain-top; he turned his eyes downward again, and, to his grief, the silver-footed Thetis had vanished in the waves. All day he sat and waited for her return, but she came not. When darkness began to fall he sought me in my cave hall, and told me what he had seen and heard; and I taught him how to win the sea nymph for his bride.

"So when the sun again gilded the crags of Pelion, brave Peleus hid himself among the rocks close by the sea-washed shore, and waited for the coming of the silver-footed lady of the sea. In a little time she rose, beautiful as the star of morning, from the waves. She sat down upon the beach, and dallied with her golden tresses, and sang sweet songs of a happy land in the depths of the sounding sea. Peleus, bearing in mind what I had taught him, arose from his hiding-place, and caught the beauteous creature in his arms. In vain did she struggle to leap into the waves. Seven times she changed her form as he held her: by turns she changed into a fountain of water, into a cloud of mist, into a burning flame, and into a senseless rock. But Peleus held her fast; and she changed then into a tawny lion, and then into a tall tree, and lastly she took her own matchless form again.

"Then Peleus held the lovely Thetis by the hand, and they walked long time together upon the beach, while the birds sang among the trees on Pelion's leafy slopes, and the dolphins sported in the waters at their feet. Thus Peleus wooed the silver-footed lady, and won her love, and she promised to be his bride. Then the immortals were glad; and they fitted up the great cavern on Mount Pelion for a banquet hall, and made therein a wedding feast, such as was never seen before. The vaulted roof of the cavern was decked with gems which shone like the stars of heaven; a thousand torches, held by lovely mountain nymphs, flamed from the niches in the high walls; and upon the floor of polished marble, tables for a thousand guests were ranged.

"When the wedding feast was ready, all those who live on high Olympus, and all the immortals who dwell upon the earth, came to rejoice with King Peleus and his matchless bride; and they brought rich presents for the bridegroom, such as were never given to another man. One gave him a suit of armor, rich and fair, a wonder to behold, which lame Vulcan with rare skill had wrought and fashioned. One bestowed on him the peerless horses, Ballos and Xanthos, and a deftly wrought chariot with trimmings of gold. And I, one of the least of the guests, gave him an ashen spear which I had cut on the mountain top and fashioned with my own hands.

"At the tables sat Zeus, the father of gods and men; and

his wife, the white-armed Hera; and smile-loving Aphrodite; and gray-eyed Athena; and all the wisest and the fairest of the immortals. The nymphs of the sea danced in honor of Thetis their sister; and the Muses sang their sweetest songs; and Apollo played upon the lyre. The Fates, too, were there: sad Clotho, twirling her spindle; unloving Lachesis, with wrinkled lips ready to speak the fatal word; and pitiless Atropos, holding in her hand the unsparing shears. And around the table passed the youthful and joy-giving Hebe, pouring out rich draughts of nectar for the guests.

"But there was one among all the immortals who had not been invited to the wedding; it was Eris, the daughter of War and Hate. Her scowling features, and her hot and hasty manners, were ill suited to grace a feast where all should be mirth and gladness; yet in her evil heart she planned to be avenged for the slight which had been put upon her. While the merry-making was at its height, and the company were listening to the music from Apollo's lyre, she came unseen into the hall, and threw a golden apple upon the table. No one knew whence the apple came; but on it were written these words, 'FOR THE FAIREST.'

"'To whom does it belong?' asked Zeus, stroking his brows in sad perplexity.

"The music ceased, and mirth and jollity fled at once from the banquet. The torches, which lit up the scene, flickered and smoked; the lustre of the gems in the vaulted roof was dimmed; dark clouds canopied the great hall: for Eris had taken her place at the table, uninvited and unwelcome though she was.

"'The apple belongs to me,' said Hera, trying to snatch it; 'for I am the queen, and gods and men honor me as having no peer on earth.'

"'Not so!' cried red-lipped Aphrodite. 'With me dwell Love and Joy; and not only do gods and men sing my praises, but all nature rejoices in my presence. The apple is mine, and I will have it!'

"Then Athena joined in the quarrel. 'What is it to be a queen,' said she, 'if at the same time one lacks that good temper which sweetens life? What is it to have a handsome form and face, while the mind is uncouth and ill-looking? Beauty of mind is better than beauty of face; for the former is immortal, while the latter fades and dies. Hence no one has a better right than I to be called the fairest.'

"Then the strife spread among the guests in the hall, each taking sides with the one he loved best; and, where peace and merriment had reigned, now hot words and bitter wrangling were heard. And had not Zeus bidden them keep silence, thus putting an end to the quarrel, all Pelion would have been rent, and the earth shaken to its centre in the mellay that would have followed.

"'Let us waste no words over this matter,' he said. 'It is not for the immortals to say who of their number is most beautiful. But on the slopes of Mount Ida, far across the sea, the fairest of the sons of men - Paris, a prince of Troy - keeps his flocks; let him judge who is fairest, and let the apple be hers to whom he gives it.'

"Then Hermes, the swift-footed messenger, arose, and led the three goddesses over sea and land to distant Mount Ida, where Paris, with no thought of the wonderful life which lay before him, piped on his shepherd's reeds, and tended his flock of sheep."

[1]Cheiron the Centaur lived in a cavern on Mount Pelion and was reputed to be the wisest of mortals. All the young heroes of the time, Jason, Achilles, and others, were his pupils and spent their boyhood with him. He is sometimes represented as having the head of a man and the body of a horse; but it is probable that he was only one of a race of men noted for their skill in horsemanship. This story is supposed to have been related by him to young Odysseus (Ulysses), who visited him in his cavern.

James Baldwin

PARIS AND CENONE

RELATED BY CHEIRON THE CENTAUR

"On the other side of the sea there stands a city, rich and mighty, the like of which there is none in Greece. The name of this city is Troy, although its inhabitants call it Ilios. There an old man, named Priam, rules over a happy and peace-loving people. He dwells in a great palace of polished marble, on a hill overlooking the plain; and his granaries are stored with corn, and his flocks and herds are pastured on the hills and mountain slopes behind the city.

"Many sons has King Priam; and they are brave and noble youths, well worthy of such a father. The eldest of these sons is Hector, who, the Trojans hope, will live to bring great honor to his native land.

"Just before the second son was born, a strange thing troubled the family of old Priam. The queen dreamed that her babe had turned into a firebrand, which burned up the walls and the high towers of Troy, and left but smouldering ashes where once the proud city stood. She told the king her dream; and when the child was born, they called a soothsayer, who could foresee the mysteries of the future, and they asked him what the vision meant.

"'It means,' said he, 'that this babe, if he lives, shall be a firebrand in Troy, and shall turn its walls and its high towers into heaps of smouldering ashes.'

"'But what shall be done with the child, that he may not do this terrible thing?' asked Priam, greatly sorrowing, for the babe was very beautiful.

"'Do not suffer that he shall live,' answered the soothsayer.

"Priam, the gentlest and most kind-hearted of men, could not bear to harm the babe. So he called his master shepherd, and bade him take the helpless child into the thick woods, which grow high up on the slopes of Mount Ida, behind the city, and there to leave him alone. The wild beasts that roam among those woods, he thought, would doubtless find him, or, in any case, he could not live long without care and nourishment; and thus the dangerous brand would be quenched while yet it was scarcely a spark.

"The shepherd did as he was bidden, although it cost his heart many a sharp pang thus to deal barbarously with the innocent. He laid the smiling infant, wrapped in its broidered tunic, close by the foot of anoak, and then hurried away that he might not hear its cries.

"But the nymphs who haunt the woods and groves, saw the babe, and pitied its helplessness, and cared for it so that it did not die. Some brought it yellow honey from the stores of the wild bees; some fed it with milk from the white goats that pastured on the mountain side; and others stood as sentinels around it, guarding it from the wolves and bears.

"Thus five days passed, and then the shepherd, who could not forget the babe, came cautiously to the spot to see if, mayhap, even its broidered cloak had been spared by the

James Baldwin

beasts. Sorrowful and shuddering he glanced toward the foot of the tree. To his surprise, the babe was still there; it looked up and smiled, and stretched its fat hands toward him. The shepherd's heart would not let him turn away the second time. He took the child in his arms, and carried it to his own humble home in the valley, where he cared for it and brought it up as his own son.

"The boy grew to be very tall and very handsome; and he was so brave, and so helpful to the shepherds around Mount Ida, that they called him Alexandros, or the helper of men; but his foster-father named him Paris. As he tended his sheep in the mountain dells, he met Oenone, the fairest of the river maidens, guileless and pure as the waters of the stream by whose banks she loved to wander. Day after day he sat with her in the shadow of her woodland home, and talked of innocence and beauty, and of a life of sweet contentment, and of love; and the maiden listened to him with wide-open eyes and a heart full of trustfulness and faith.

"By and by, Paris and Oenone were wedded; and their little cottage in the mountain glen was the fairest and happiest spot in Ilios. The days sped swiftly by, and neither of them dreamed that any sorrow was in store for them; and to Oenone her shepherd husband was all the world, because he was so noble and brave and handsome and gentle.

"One warm summer afternoon, Paris sat in the shade of a tree at the foot of Mount Ida, while his flocks were pasturing upon the hillside before him. The bees were humming lazily among the flowers; the cicadas were chirping among the leaves above his head; and now and then a bird twittered softly among the bushes behind him. All else was still, as if enjoying to the full the delicious calm of that pleasant day.

"Paris was fashioning a slender reed into a shepherd's flute; while Oenone, sitting in the deeper shadows of some clustering vines, was busy with some simple piece of needlework.

"A sound as of sweet music caused the young shepherd to raise his eyes. Before him stood the four immortals, Hera, Athena, Aphrodite, and Hermes the messenger; their faces shone with a dazzling radiance, and they were fairer than any tongue can describe. At their feet rare flowers sprang up, crocuses and asphodels and white lilies; and the air was filled with the odor of orange blossoms. Paris, scarce knowing what he did, arose to greet them. No handsomer youth ever stood in the presence of beauty. Straight as a mountain pine was he; a leopard-skin hung carelessly upon his shoulders; his head was bare, but his locks clustered round his temples in sunny curls, and formed fit framework for his fair brows.

"Hermes spoke first: 'Paris, we have come to seek thy help; there is strife among the folk who dwell on Mount Olympus. Here are Hera, Athena, and Aphrodite, each claiming to be the fairest, and each clamoring for this prize, this golden apple. Now we pray that you will judge this matter, and give the apple to the one whom you may deem most beautiful.'

"Then Hera began her plea at once: 'I know that I am fairest,' she said, 'for I am queen, and mine it is to rule among gods and men. Give me the prize, and you shall have wealth, and a kingdom, and great glory; and men in aftertimes shall sing your praises.'

"And Paris was half tempted to give the apple, without further ado, to Hera, the proud queen. But gray-eyed Athena spoke: 'There is that, fair youth, which is better than riches or honor or great glory. Listen to me, and I will give thee wisdom and a pure heart; and thy life shall be crowned with peace, and sweetened with love, and made strong by knowledge. And though men may not sing of thee in after-times, thou shall find lasting happiness in the answer of a good conscience towards all things."

"Then Oenone whispered from her place among the leaves, 'Give the prize to Athena; she is the fairest.' And Paris would have placed the golden apple in her hand, had not Aphrodite stepped quickly forward, and in the sweetest, merriest tones, addressed him.

"'You may look at my face, and judge for yourself as to whether I am fair,' said she laughing, and tossing her curls. 'All I shall say is this: Give me the prize, and you shall have for your wife the most beautiful woman in the world.'

"The heart of Oenone stood still as Paris placed the apple in Aphrodite's hand; and a nameless dread came over her, as if the earth were sinking beneath her feet. But the next moment the blood came back to her cheeks, and she breathed free and strong again; for she heard Paris say, 'I have a wife, Oenone, who to me is the loveliest of mortals, and I care not for your offer; yet I give to you the apple, for I know that you are the fairest among the deathless ones who live on high Olympus.'"

"On the very next day it happened that King Priam sat thoughtfully in his palace, and all his boys and girls - nearly fifty in number - were about him. His mind turned sadly to the little babe whom he had sent away, many years ago, to die alone on wooded Ida. And he said to himself, 'The child has been long dead, and yet no feast has been given to the gods that they may make his little spirit glad in the shadowy land of Hades. This must not be neglected longer. Within three days a feast must be made, and we will hold games in his honor.'

"Then he called his servants, and bade them go to the pastures on Mount Ida, and choose from the herds that were there the fattest and handsomest bull, to be given as a prize to the winner in the games. And he proclaimed through all Ilios, that on the third day there would be a great feast in his palace, and games would be held in honor of the little babe who had died twenty years before.

"Now, when the servants came to Mount Ida, they chose a bull for which Paris had long cared, and which he loved more than any other. He protested and would not let the beast be driven from the pasture until it was agreed that he might go to the city with it and contend in the games for the prize. But Oenone, the river nymph, wept and prayed him not to go.

"'Leave not the pleasant pasture lands of Ida, even for a day,' said she; 'for my heart tells me that you will not return.'

"'Think not so, my fair one,' said Paris. 'Did not Aphrodite promise that the most beautiful woman in the world shall be my wife? And who is more beautiful than my own Oenone? Dry now your tears; for when I have won the prizes in the games I will come back to you, and never leave you again.'

"Then the grief of Oenone waxed still greater. 'If you will go,' she cried, 'then hear my warning! Long years shall pass ere you shall come again to wooded Ida, and the hearts which now are young shall grow old and feeble by reason of much sorrow. Cruel war and many dire disasters shall overtake you, and death shall be nigh unto you; and then Oenone, although long forgotten by you, will hasten

James Baldwin

to your side, to help and to heal and to forgive, that so the old love may live again. Farewell!'

"Then Paris kissed his wife, and hastened, light of heart, to Troy. How could it be otherwise but that, in the games which followed, the handsome young shepherd should carry off all the prizes?

"'Who are you?' asked the king.

"'My name is Paris,' answered the shepherd, 'and I feed the flocks and herds on wooded Ida.'

"Then Hector, full of wrath because of his own failure to win a prize, came forward to dispute with Paris.

"'Stand there, Hector,' cried old Priam; 'stand close to the young shepherd, and let us look at you!' Then turning to the queen, he asked, 'Did you ever see two so nearly alike? The shepherd is fairer and of slighter build, it is true; but they have the same eye, the same frown, the same smile, the same motion of the shoulders, the same walk. Ah, what if the young babe did not die after all?'

"Then Priam's daughter, Cassandra, who had the gift of prophecy, cried out, 'Oh, blind of eye and heart, that you cannot see in this young shepherd the child whom you sent to sleep the sleep of death on Ida's wooded slopes!'

"And so it came about, that Paris was taken into his father's house, and given the place of honor which was his by right. And he forgot Oenone, his fair young wife, and left her to pine in loneliness among the woods and in the narrow dells of sunny Ida."

HESIONE

RELATED BY MENELAUS[1]

With troubled brow and anxious heart, Menelaus sat in Nestor's halls, and told the story of his wrongs. Behind him stood his brother, Agamemnon, tall and strong, and with eye and forehead like mighty Zeus. Before him, seated on a fair embroidered couch, was the aged Nestor, listening with eager ears. Close by his feet two heroes sat: on this side, Antilochus, the valiant son of Nestor; and on that, sage Palamedes, prince of Euboea's distant shores. The last had just arrived, and had not learned the errand that had brought Menelaus hither.

"Tell again the story of your visit to Troy," said Nestor. "Our guest, good Palamedes, would fain hear it; and I doubt not that he may be of service in your cause. Tell us the whole story, for we would all know more about the famous city and its kingly rulers."

Then Menelaus began once more at the beginning.

THE STORY

There is no need that I should speak of my long voyage to Troy, or of the causes which persuaded me to undertake it. When I drew near the lofty walls of the city, and through the gate, which is called Scaean, could see the rows of stately dwellings and the busy market-place and

James Baldwin

the crowds of people, I stopped there in wonder, hesitating to venture farther.

Then I sent a herald to the gate, who should make known my name and lineage and the errand upon which I had come; but I waited without in the shade of a spreading beech, not far from the towering wall. Before me stood the mighty city; behind me the fertile plain sloped gently to the sea; on my right hand flowed the sparkling waters of the river Scamander; while much farther, and on the other side, the wooded peak of Ida lifted itself toward the clouds.

But I had not long to view this scene; for a noble company of men led by Paris himself, handsome as Apollo, came out of the gate to welcome me. With words of greeting from the king, they bade me enter within the walls. They led me through the Scaean gate and along the well-paved streets, until we came, at last, to King Priam's hall.

It was a splendid house with broad doorways and polished porticos, and marble columns richly carved. Within were fifty chambers, joining one another, all walled with polished stone; in these abode the fifty sons of Priam with their wedded wives. On the other side, and opening into the court, were twelve chambers built for his daughters; while over all were the sleeping-rooms for that noble household, and around were galleries and stairways leading to the king's great hall below.

King Priam received me kindly, and, when he understood my errand, left naught undone to help me forward with my wishes. Ten days I abode as a guest in his halls, and when I would return to Greece he pressed me to tarry yet a month in Troy. But the winds were fair, and the oracles promised a pleasant voyage, and I begged that on the twelfth day he would let me depart. So he and his sons brought many gifts, rich and beautiful, and laid them at my feet - a fair mantle, and a doublet, and a talent of fine gold, and a sword with a silver-studded hilt, and a drinking-cup richly engraved that I might remember them when I pour libations to the gods.

"Take these gifts," said Priam, "as tokens of our friendship for you, and not only for you, but for all who dwell in distant Greece. For we too are the children of the immortals. Our mighty ancestor, Dardanus, was the son of Zeus. He it was who built Dardania on the slopes of Ida, where the waters gush in many silvery streams from underneath the rocky earth.

"A grandson of Dardanus was Ilus, famous in song and story, and to him was born Laomedon, who in his old age became my father. He, though my sire, did many unwise things, and brought sore distress upon the people of this land.

"One day Apollo and Poseidon came to Troy, disguised as humble wayfarers seeking some employment. This they did because so ordered by mighty Zeus.

"'What can you do?' asked my father, when the two had told their wishes.

"Poseidon answered, 'I am a builder of walls.'

"And Apollo answered, 'I am a shepherd, and a tender of herds.'

"'It is well,' answered Laomedon. 'The wall-builder shall build a wall around this Troy so high and strong that no enemy can pass it. The shepherd shall tend my herds of crook-horned kine on the wooded slopes of Ida. If at the end of a twelvemonth, the wall be built, and if the cattle thrive without loss of one, then I will pay you your hire: a talent of gold, two tripods of silver, rich robes, and armor such as heroes wear.'

"So the two served my father through the year for the hire which he had promised. Poseidon built a wall, high and fair, around the city; and Apollo tended the shambling kine, and lost not one. But when they claimed their hire, Laomedon drove them away with threats, telling them that he would bind their feet and hands together, and sell them as slaves into some distant land, having first sheared off their ears with his sharp sword. And they went away with angry hearts, planning in their minds how they might avenge themselves.

"Back to his watery kingdom, and his golden palace beneath the sea, went great Poseidon. He harnessed his steeds to his chariot, and rode forth upon the waves. He loosed the winds from their prison house, and sent them raging over the sea. The angry waters rushed in upon the land; they covered the pastures and the rich plain of Troy, and threatened even to beat down the walls which their king had built.

"Then little by little, the flood shrank back again; and the people went out of the city to see the waste of slime and black mud which covered their meadows. While they were gazing upon the scene, a fearful monster, sent by angry Poseidon, came up out of the sea, and fell upon them, and drove them with hideous slaughter back to the city gates; neither would he allow any one to come outside of the walls.

"Then my father, in his great distress, clad himself in mourning, and went in deep humility to the temple of Athena. In much distress, he called unto the goddess, and besought to know the means whereby the anger of Poseidon might be assuaged. And in solemn tones a voice replied, saying:

"'Every day one of the maidens of Troy must be fed to the monster outside of the walls. The shaker of the earth has spoken. Disobey him not, lest more cruel punishments befall thee.'

"Then in every house of Troy there was sore dismay and lamentation, for no one knew upon whom the doom would soonest fall. And every day a hapless maiden, young and fair, was chained to the great rock by the shore, and left there to be the food of the pitiless monster. And the people cried aloud in their distress, and cursed the mighty walls and the high towers which had been reared by the unpaid labors of Poseidon; and my father sat upon his high seat, and trembled because of the calamities which his own deeds had brought upon his people.

"At last, after many humbler victims had perished, the lot fell upon the fairest of my sisters, Hesione, my father's best-loved daughter. In sorrow we arrayed her in garments befitting one doomed to an untimely death; and when we had bidden her a last farewell, we gave her to the heralds and the priests to lead forth to the place of sacrifice.

"Just then, however, a noble stranger, taller and more stately than any man in Troy, came down the street. Fair-haired and blue-eyed, handsome and strong, he seemed a very god to all who looked upon him. Over his shoulder he wore the tawny skin of a lion, while in his hand he carried a club most wonderful to behold. And the people, as he passed, prayed him that he would free our city from the monster that was robbing us of our loved ones.

James Baldwin

"'I know that thou art a god!' cried my father, when he saw the stranger. 'I pray thee, save my daughter, who even now is being led forth to a cruel death!'

"'You make mistake,' answered the fair stranger. 'I am not one of the gods. My name is Hercules, and like you I am mortal. Yet I may help you in this your time of need.'

"Now, in my father's stables there were twelve fair steeds, the best that the earth ever knew. So light of foot were they, that when they bounded over the land, they might run upon the topmost ears of ripened corn, and break them not; and when they bounded over the sea, not even Poseidon's steeds could glide so lightly upon the crests of the waves. Some say they were the steeds of North Wind given to my grandfather by the powers above. These steeds, my father promised to give to Hercules if he would save Hesione.

"Then the heralds led my fair sister to the shore, and chained her to the rock, there to wait for the coming of the monster. But Hercules stood near her, fearless in his strength. Soon the waves began to rise; the waters were disturbed, and the beast, with hoarse bellowings, lifted his head above the breakers, and rushed forward to seize his prey. Then the hero sprang to meet him. With blow upon blow from his mighty club, he felled the monster; the waters of the sea were reddened with blood; Hesione was saved, and Troy was freed from the dreadful curse.

"'Behold thy daughter!' said Hercules, leading her gently back to the city, and giving her to her father. 'I have saved her from the jaws of death, and delivered your country from the dread scourge. Give me now my hire.'

"Shame fills my heart as I tell this story, for thanklessness was the bane of my father's life. Ungrateful to the hero who had risked so much and done so much that our homes and our country might be saved from ruin, he turned coldly away from Hercules; then he shut the great gates in his face, and barred him out of the city, and taunted him from the walls, saying, 'I owe thee no hire! Begone from our coasts, ere I scourge thee hence!'

"Full of wrath, the hero turned away. 'I go, but I will come again,' he said.

"Then peace and plenty blessed once more the city of Troy, and men forgot the perils from which they had been delivered. But ere long, great Hercules returned, as he had promised; and with him came a fleet of white-sailed ships and many warriors. Neither gates nor strong walls could stand against him. Into the city he marched, and straight to my father's palace. All fled before him, and the strongest warriors quailed beneath his glance. Here, in this very court, he slew my father and my brothers with his terrible arrows. I myself would have fallen before his wrath, had not my sister, fair Hesione, pleaded for my life.

"'I spare his life,' said Hercules, in answer to her prayers, 'for he is but a lad. Yet he must be my slave until you have paid a price for him, and thus redeemed him.'

"Then Hesione took the golden veil from her head, and gave it to the hero as my purchase price. And thenceforward I was called Priam, or the purchased; for the name which my mother gave me was Podarkes, or the fleet-footed.

"After this Hercules and his heroes went on board their ships and sailed back across the sea, leaving me alone in my father's halls. For they took fair Hesione with them, and carried her to Salamis, to be the wife of Telamon, the father of mighty Ajax. There, through these long years she has lived in sorrow, far removed from home and friends and the scenes of her happy childhood. And now that the hero Telamon, to whom she was wedded, lives no longer, I ween that her life is indeed a cheerless one."

"When Priam had finished his tale, he drew his seat still nearer mine, and looked into my face with anxious, beseeching eyes. Then he said, 'I have long wished to send a ship across the sea to bring my sister back to Troy. A dark-prowed vessel, built for speed and safety, lies now at anchor in the harbor, and a picked crew is ready to embark at any moment. And here is my son Paris, handsome and brave, who is anxious to make voyage to Salamis, to seek unhappy Hesione. Yet our seamen have never ventured far from home, and they know nothing of the dangers of the deep, nor do they feel sure they can find their way to Greece. And so we have a favor to ask of you; and that is, that when your ship sails to-morrow, ours may follow in its wake across the sea."

Here Menelaus paused as if in deep thought, and not until his listeners begged him to go on, did he resume his story.

[1]Menelaus, king of Lacedaemon, was the husband of Helen, the most beautiful woman in the world. At the time of his marriage to Helen all the princes of Greece had vowed to support him against any enemy who should attempt to defraud him of his rights. This and the following story tell of his visit to Troy and its results.

PARIS AND HELEN

MENELAUS CONTINUES HIS STORY

"I was glad when King Priam made this request," continued Menelaus, "for, in truth, I was loath to part with Paris; and I arranged at once that he should bear me company in my own ship while his vessel with its crew followed not far behind.

"And so, being blessed with favoring winds, we made a quick voyage back to my own country. What followed is too sad for lengthy mention, and is in part already known to you. Need I tell you how I opened my halls to Paris, and left no act of courtesy undone that I might make him happy? Need I tell you how he was welcomed by fair Helen, and how the summer days fled by on golden wings; and how in the delights of Lacedaemon he forgot his errand to Salamis, and cared only to remain with me, my honored guest and trusted friend?

"One day a message came to me from my old friend Idomeneus. He had planned a hunt among the mountains and woods of Crete, and he invited me to join him in the sport. I had not seen Idomeneus since the time that we together, in friendly contention, sought the hand of Helen. I could not do otherwise than accept his invitation, for he had sent his own ship to carry me over to Crete.

"So I bade farewell to Helen, saying, 'Let not our noble

James Baldwin

guest lack entertainment while I am gone; and may the golden hours glide happily until I come again.' And to Paris I said, 'Tarry another moon in Lacedasmon; and when I return from Crete, I will go with you to Salamis, and aid you in your search for Hesione.'

"Then I went on board the waiting ship, and prospering breezes carried us without delays to Crete.

"Idomeneus received me joyfully, and entertained me most royally in his palace; and for nine days we feasted and made all things ready for the hunt. But, lo! on the evening of the last day, a vision came to me. Gold-winged Iris, the fleet-footed messenger of the gods, stood before me. 'Hasten back to Lacedaemon,' she cried, for thou art robbed of thy dearest treasure!' And even while she spoke, one of my own ships, came sailing into the harbor, bringing trusted heralds whom the elders of Lacedaemon had sent to me.

"They told me the fatal news. 'No sooner were you well on your way,' they said, 'than Paris began to put his ship in readiness to depart. Helen prayed him to tarry until your return, but he would not hearken, "I will stay no longer," he said. "My seamen rest upon their oars; the sails of my ship are spread; the breeze will soon spring up that will carry me across the sea. But you, beauteous Helen, shall go with me; for the deathless gods have spoken it. Aphrodite, long ago, promised that the most beautiful woman in the world should be my wife. And who is that most beautiful woman if it be not yourself? Come! fly over the sea, and be my queen. It is the will of the gods.'"

"It was thus that the perfidious Trojan wrought the ruin of all that was dear to me.

"At first, Helen refused. But Paris is a handsome prince, and day after day he renewed his suit. Then on the sixth day she yielded. In the darkness of the night they went on board his waiting vessel, carrying with them the gold and jewels of my treasure house; and in the morning, when the sun arose on Lacedaemon, they were far out at sea.

"You know the rest: how in wrath and great sorrow I hurried home; how I first counselled with my own elders, and then with my brother Agamemnon. And now, O noble Nestor, we have come to Pylos, seeking thy advice. On these two things my mind is set: Helen must be mine again, and Paris must suffer the punishment due to traitors."

When Menelaus had ended, sage Nestor answered with many words of counsel. "Keep the thought of vengeance ever before you," he said. "Yet act not rashly. The power of Troy is very great; and, in case of war, all the tribes of Asia will make common cause with her. But an insult to Lacedaemon is an insult to all Greece, and every loyal Greek will hasten to avenge it. More than this, the chiefs of almost every state have already sworn to aid you. We have but to call upon them, and remind them of their oaths, and the mightiest warriors of our land will take up arms against the power of Troy."

James Baldwin

IPHIGENIA

After nearly ten years of preparation, the princes and warriors of Greece gathered their ships and men together at Aulis, ready to make war upon Troy. A thousand dark-hulled vessels were moored in the harbor; and a hundred thousand brave men were on board, ready to follow their leaders whithersoever they should order.

Chief of all that host was mighty Agamemnon, king of men. He was clad in flashing armor, and his mind was filled with overweening pride when he thought how high he stood among the warriors, and that his men were the goodliest and bravest of all that host.

Next to him was Menelaus, silent and discreet, by no means skilled above his fellows, and yet, by reason of his noble heart, beloved and honored by all the Greeks; and it was to avenge his wrongs that this mighty array of men and ships had been gathered together.

Odysseus came next, shrewd in counsels, earnest and active. He moved among the men and ships, inspiring all with zeal and courage.

There, also, was young Achilles, tall and handsome, and swift of foot. His long hair fell about his shoulders like a shower of gold, and his gray eyes gleamed like those of the mountain eagle. By the shore lay his trim ships - fifty in all - with thousands of gallant warriors on board.

One day it chanced that Agamemnon, while hunting, started a fine stag, and gave it a long chase among the hills and through the wooded dells, until it sought safety in a grove sacred to Artemis, the huntress queen. The proud king knew that this was a holy place, where beasts and birds might rest secure from harm; yet he cared naught for what Artemis had ordained, and with his swift arrows he slew the panting deer.

Then was the huntress queen moved with anger, and she declared that the ships of the Greeks should not sail from Aulis until the king had atoned for his crime. A great calm rested upon the sea, and not a breath of air stirred the sails at the mast-heads of the ships.

Day after day and week after week went by, and not a speck of cloud was seen in the sky above, and not a ripple on the glassy face of the deep. All the ships had been put in order, new vessels had been built, the warriors had burnished their armor and overhauled their arms a thousand times; and yet no breeze arose to waft them across the sea. And they began to murmur, and to talk bitterly against Agamemnon and the chiefs.

At last Agamemnon sent for Calchas, the soothsayer, and asked him in secret how the anger of the huntress queen might be appeased. And the soothsayer with tears and lamentations answered that in no wise could it be done save by the sacrifice to Artemis of the king's daughter, Iphigenia.

Then the king cried aloud in his grief, and declared that though Troy might stand forever, he would not do that thing; and he bade a herald go through the camp, and among the ships by the shore, and bid every man depart as he chose to his own country. But before the herald had gone from his tent, behold, his brother, Menelaus, stood

James Baldwin

before him with downcast eyes and saddest of hearts.

"After ten years of labor and hope," said he to Agamemnon, "wouldst thou give up this enterprise, and lose all?"

Then Odysseus came also into the tent, and added his persuasions to those of Menelaus. The king hearkened to him, for no man was more crafty in counsel; and the three recalled the herald, and formed a plan whereby they might please Artemis by doing as she desired. Agamemnon, in his weakness, wrote a letter to Clytemnestra his queen, telling her to bring the maiden, Iphigenia, to Aulis, there to be wedded to the bravest of all the Greeks.

"*Fail not in this,*" added he, "*for the godlike hero will not sail with us unless my daughter be given to him in marriage.*"

And when he had written the letter, he sealed it, and sent it by a swift messenger to Clytemnestra at Mycenas.

Nevertheless the king's heart was full of sorrow, and when he was alone he planned how he might yet save his daughter. Night came, but he could not sleep; he walked the floor of his tent; he wept and lamented like one bereft of reason. At length he sat down, and wrote another letter:

"*Daughter of Leda, send not thy child to Aulis, for I will give her in marriage at another time.*"

Then he called another messenger, an old and trusted servant of the household, and put this letter into his hands.

"Take this with all haste to my queen, who, perchance, is even now on her way to Aulis. Stop not by any cool spring in the groves, and let not thine eyes close for sleep.

And see that the chariot bearing the queen and Iphigenia pass thee not unnoticed."

The messenger took the letter and hastened away. But hardly had he passed the line of the tents when Menelaus saw him, and took the letter away from him. And when he had read it, he went before his brother, and reproached him| with bitter words.

"Before you were chosen captain of the host," said he, "you were kind and gentle, and the friend of every man. There was nothing that you would not do to aid your fellows. Now you are puffed up with pride and vain conceit, and care nothing even for those who are your equals in power. Yet, for all, you are not rid of your well-known cowardice; and when you saw that your leadership was likely to be taken away from you unless you obeyed the commands of Artemis, you agreed to do this thing. Now you are trying to break your word, sending secretly to your wife, and bidding her not to bring her daughter to Aulis."

Then Agamemnon answered, "Why should I destroy my daughter in order to win back thy wife? Let those who wish go with thee to Troy. In no way am I bound to serve thee."

"Do as you will," said Menelaus, going away in wrath.

Soon after this, there came a herald to the king, saying, "Behold, your daughter Iphigenia has come as you directed, and with her mother and her little brother Orestes she rests by the spring close to the outer line of tents. The warriors have gathered around them, and are praising her loveliness, and asking many questions; and some say, 'The king is sick to see his daughter, whom he loves so deeply, and he has made up some excuse to bring her to the camp.' But I know why you have brought her here; for I have been told about the wedding, and the noble groom who is to lead her in marriage; and we will rejoice and be glad, because this is a happy day for the maiden."

Then the king was sorely distressed, and knew not what to do. "Sad, sad, indeed," said he, "is the wedding to which the maiden cometh. For the name of the bridegroom is Death."

At the same time Menelaus came back, sorrowful and repentant. "You were right, my brother," said he. "What, indeed, has Iphigenia to do with this enterprise, and why should the maiden die for me? Send the Greeks to their homes, and let not this great wrong be done."

"But how can I do that now?" asked Agamemnon. "The warriors, urged on by Odysseus and Calchas, will force me to do the deed. Or, if I flee to Mycenae, they will follow me, and slay me, and destroy my city. Oh, woe am I, that such a day should ever dawn upon my sight!"

Even while they spoke together, the queen's chariot drove up to the tent door, and the queen and Iphigenia and the little Orestes alighted quickly, and merrily greeted the king.

"It is well that you have sent for me, my father," said Iphigenia, caressing him.

"It may be well, and yet it may not," said Agamemnon. "I am exceeding glad to see thee alive and happy."

"If you are glad, why then do you weep?"

"I am sad because thou wilt be so long time away from me."

"Are you going on a very long voyage, father?"

"A long voyage and a sad one, my child. And thou, also, hast a journey to make."

"Must I make it alone, or will my mother go with me?"

"Thou must make it alone. Neither father nor mother nor any friend can go with thee, my child."

"But when shall it be? I pray that you will hasten this matter with Troy, and return home ere then."

"It may be so. But I must offer a sacrifice to the gods before we sail from Aulis."

"That is well. And may I be present?"
"Yes, and thou shalt be very close to the altar."

"Shall I lead in the dances, father?"

Then the king could say no more, for reason of the great sorrow within him; and he kissed the maiden, and sent her into the tent. A little while afterward, the queen came and spoke to him and asked him about the man to whom their daughter was to be wedded; and Agamemnon, still dissembling, told her that the hero's name was Achilles, and that he was the son of old Peleus and the sea-nymph Thetis.

"And when and where is the marriage to be?" asked the queen.

"On the first lucky day in the present moon, and here in our camp at Aulis," answered Agamemnon.

"Shall I stay here with thee until then?"

James Baldwin

"Nay, thou must go back to Mycenae without delay."

"But may I not come again? If I am not here, who will hold up the torch for the bride?"

"I will attend to all such matters," answered Agamemnon.

But Clytemnestra was not well pleased, neither could the king persuade her at all that she should return to Mycenae. While yet they were talking, Achilles himself came to the tent door, and said aloud to the servant who kept it, "Tell thy master that Achilles, the son of Peleus, would be pleased to see him."

When Clytemnestra overheard these words, she hastened to the door, and offered the hero her hand. But he was abashed and drew back, for it was deemed an unseemly thing for men to speak thus with women. Then Clytemnestra said, "Why, indeed, should you, who are about to marry my daughter, be ashamed to give me your hand?"

Achilles was struck with wonder, and asked her what she meant; and when she had explained the matter, he said:

"Truly I have never been a suitor for thy daughter, neither has Agamemnon or Menelaus spoken a word to me regarding her."

And now the queen was astonished in her turn, and cried out with shame that she had been so cruelly deceived. Then the keeper of the door, who was the same that had been sent with the letter, came forward and told the truth regarding the whole matter. And Clytemnestra cried to Achilles, "O son of silver-footed Thetis! Help me and help my daughter Iphigenia, in this time of sorest need! For we have no friend in all this host, and none in whom we can confide but thee."

Achilles answered, "Long time ago I was a pupil of old Cheiron, the most righteous of men, and from him I learned to be honest and true. If Agamemnon rule according to right, then I will obey him; but not otherwise. And now, since thy daughter was brought to this place under pretence of giving her to me as my bride, I will see that she shall not be slain, neither shall any one dare take her from me."

On the following day, while Agamemnon sat grief-stricken in his tent, the maiden came before him carrying the child Orestes in her arms; and she cast herself upon her knees at his feet, and caressing his hands, she thus besought him:

"Would, dear father, that I had the voice of Orpheus, to whom even the rocks did listen! then I would persuade thee. O father! I am thy child. I was the first to call thee 'Father,' and the first to whom thou saidst 'My child.'"

The father turned his face away, and wept; he could not speak for sadness. Then the maiden went on: "O father, hear me! thou to whom my voice was once so sweet that thou wouldst waken me to hear my prattle. And when I was older grown, then thou wouldst say to me, 'Some day, my birdling, thou shalt have a nest of thy own, a home of which thou shalt be the mistress.' And I did answer, 'Yes, dear father, and when thou art old I will care for thee, and pay thee with all my heart for the kindness thou dost show me.' But now thou hast forgotten it all, and art ready to slay my young life."

A deep groan burst from the lips of the mighty king, but he spoke not a word. Then, after a deathlike silence broken only by the deep breathings of father and child, Iphigenia spoke again: "My father, can there be any prayer more pure and more persuasive than that of a

James Baldwin

maiden for her father's welfare? And when, the cruel knife shall strike me down, thou wilt have one daughter less to pray for thee." A shudder shook the frame of Agamemnon, but he answered not a word.

At that moment Achilles entered. He had come in haste from the tents beside the shore, and he spoke in hurried, anxious accents.

"Behold," said he, "a great tumult has arisen in the camp; for Calchas has given out among the men that you refuse to do what Artemis has bidden, and that hence these delays and troubles have arisen. And the rude soldiers are crying out against you, and declaring that the maiden must die. When I would have stayed their anger, they took up stones to stone me - my own warriors among the rest. And now they are making ready to move upon your tent, threatening to sacrifice you also with your daughter. But I will fight for you to the utmost, and the maiden shall not die."

As he was speaking, Calchas entered, and, grasping the wrist of the pleading maiden, lifted her to her feet. She looked up, and saw his stony face and hard cold eyes; and turning again to Agamemnon, she said, "O father, the ships shall sail, for I will die for thee."

Then Achilles said to her, "Fair maiden, thou art by far the noblest and most lovely of thy sex. Fain would I save thee from this fate, even though every man in Greece be against me. Fly with me quickly to my long-oared ship, and I will carry thee safely away from this accursed place."

"Not so," answered Iphigenia: "I will give up my life for my father and this land of the Greeks, and no man shall suffer for me."

Then the pitiless priest led her through the throng of rude soldiers to the grove of Artemis, wherein an altar had been built. But Achilles and Agamemnon covered their faces with their mantles, and stayed inside the tent.

As the maiden took her place upon the altar, the king's herald stood up, and bade the warriors keep silence; and Calchas put a garland of sweet-smelling flowers about the victim's head.

"Let no man touch me," said the maiden, "for I offer my neck to the sword with right good will, that so my father may live and prosper."

In silence and great awe, the warriors stood around, while Calchas drew a sharp knife from its scabbard. But, lo! as he struck, the maiden was not there; and in her stead, a noble deer lay dying on the altar. Then the old soothsayer cried out in triumphant tones, "See, now, ye men of Greece, how the gods have provided for you a sacrifice, and saved the innocent daughter of the king!" And all the people shouted with joy; and in that self-same hour, a strong breeze came down the bay, and filled the idle sails of the waiting ships.

"To Troy! to Troy!" cried the Greeks; and every man hastened aboard his vessel.

How it was that fair Iphigenia escaped the knife; by whom she was saved, or whither she went - no one knew. Some say that Artemis carried her away to the land of the Taurians, where she had a temple and an altar; and there is a story that, long years afterward, her brother Orestes found her there, and led her back to her girlhood's home, even to Mycenae. But whether this be true or not, I know that there have been maidens as noble, as loving, as innocent as she, who have given up their lives in order to make this world a purer and happier place in which to live; and these are not dead, but live in the grateful memories of those whom they loved and saved.

THE HOARD OF THE ELVES

REGIN'S STORY[1]

When the earth was still very young, and men were feeble and few, and the Dwarfs were many and strong, the Asa-folk were wont oft-times to leave their halls in heaven-towering Asgard in order to visit the new-formed mid-world, and to see what the short-lived sons of men were doing. Sometimes they came in their own god-like splendor and might; sometimes they came disguised as feeble men folk, with all man's weaknesses and all his passions. Sometimes Odin, as a beggar, wandered from one country to another, craving charity; sometimes, as a warrior clad in coat of mail, he rode forth to battle for the cause of right; or as a minstrel he sang from door to door, and played sweet music in the halls of the great; or as a huntsman he dashed through brakes and fens, and into dark forests, and climbed steep mountains in search of game; or as a sailor he embarked upon the sea, and sought new scenes in unknown lands. And many times did men folk entertain him unawares.

Once on a time he came to the mid-world in company with Hoenir and Loki; and the three wandered through many lands and in many climes, each giving gifts wherever they went. Odin gave knowledge and strength, and taught men how to read the mystic runes; Hoenir gave gladness and good cheer, and lightened many hearts with the glow of his comforting presence; but Loki had naught

James Baldwin

to give but cunning deceit and base thoughts, and he left behind him bitter strife and many aching breasts.

At last, growing tired of the fellowship of men, the three Asas sought the solitude of the forest, and as huntsmen wandered long among the hills and over the wooded heights of Hunaland. Late one afternoon they came to a mountain stream at a place where it poured over a ledge of rocks and fell in clouds of spray into a rocky gorge below. As they stood, and with pleased eyes gazed upon the waterfall, they saw near the bank an otter lazily making ready to eat a salmon which he had caught. Then Loki, ever bent on doing mischief, hurled a stone at the harmless beast, and killed it. And he boasted loudly that he had done a worthy deed. He took both the otter and the fish which it had caught, and carried them with him as trophies of the day's success.

Just at nightfall the three huntsmen came to a lone farmhouse in the valley, and asked for food, and for shelter during the night.

"Shelter you shall have," said the farmer, whose name was Hreidmar, "for the rising clouds foretell a storm. But food I have none to give you. Surely huntsmen of skill should not want for food, since the forest teems with game, and the streams are full of fish."

Then Loki threw upon the ground the otter and the fish, and said, "We have sought in both forest and stream, and we have taken from them at one blow both flesh and fish. Give us but the shelter you promise, and we will not trouble you for food."

The farmer gazed with horror upon the lifeless body of the otter and cried out, "This creature which you mistook for an otter, and which you have robbed and killed, is my son, Oddar, who for mere pastime had taken the form of the furry beast. You are but thieves and murderers!"

Then he called loudly for help: and his two sons, Fafnir and Regin, sturdy and valiant kin of the dwarf-folk, rushed in, and seized upon the huntsmen, and bound them hand and foot; for the three Asas, having taken upon themselves the forms of men, had no more than human strength, and were unable to withstand them.

Then Odin and his fellows bemoaned their ill fate. And Loki said, "Wherefore did we foolishly take upon ourselves the likenesses of puny men? Had I my own power once more, I would never part with it in exchange for man's weaknesses."

And Hoenir sighed, and said, "Now, indeed, will darkness win: and the frosty breath of the Northern giants will blast the fair handiwork of the sunlight and the heat; for the givers of life and light and warmth are helpless prisoners in the hands of these cunning and unforgiving jailers."

"Surely," said Odin, "not even the highest are free from obedience to heaven's behests and the laws of right. I, whom men call the Preserver of Life, have debased myself by being found in evil company; and, although I have done no other wrong, I suffer rightly for the doings of this mischief-maker with whom I have stooped to have fellowship. For all are known, not so much by what they are as by what they seem to be, and they bear the bad name which their comrades bear. Now I am fallen from my high estate. Eternal right is higher than I."

Then the Asas asked Hreidmar, their jailer, what ransom they should pay for their freedom; and he, not knowing who they were, said, "I must first know what ransom you are able to give."

"We will give you anything you may ask," hastily answered Loki.

Hreidmar then called his sons, and bade them strip the skin from the otter's body. When this was done, they brought the furry hide and spread it upon the ground; and Hreidmar said, "Bring shining gold and precious stones enough to cover every part of this otter skin. When you have paid so much ransom, you shall have your freedom." "That we will do," answered Odin. "But one of us must have leave to go and fetch it: the other two will stay fast bound until the morning dawns. If, by that time, the gold is not here, you may do with us as you please."

Hreidmar and the two young men agreed to Odin's offer; and, lots being cast, it fell to Loki to go and fetch the treasure. When he had been loosed from the cords which bound him, Loki donned his magic shoes, which had carried him over land and sea from the farthest bounds of the mid-world, and hastened away upon his errand. And he sped with the swiftness of light, over the hills and the wooded slopes, and the deep dark valleys, and the fields and forests and sleeping hamlets, until he came to the place where dwelt the swarthy elves and the cunning dwarf Andvari. There the River Rhine, no larger than a meadow brook, breaks forth from beneath a mountain of ice, which the Frost giants and the Winter-king had built long years before; for they had vainly hoped that they might imprison the river at its fountain head. But the baby brook had eaten its way beneath the frozen mass, and had sprung out from its prison, and gone on, leaping and smiling, and kissing the sunlight, in its ever-widening course toward the distant sea.

Loki came to this place, because he knew that here was the home of the elves who had laid up the greatest hoard of treasures ever known in the mid-world. He scanned with careful eyes the mountain side, and the deep, rocky caverns, and the dark gorge through which the little river rushed; but in the dim moonlight not a living being could he see, save a lazy salmon swimming in the quieter eddies of the stream. Anyone but Loki would have lost all hope of finding treasure there, at least before the dawn of day; but his wits were quick and his eyes were very sharp.

"One salmon has brought us into this trouble, and another shall help us out of it!" he cried.

Then, swift as thought, he sprang again into the air; and the magic shoes carried him with greater speed than before down the Rhine valley, and through Burgundyland and the low meadows, until he came to the shores of the great North Sea. He sought the halls of old Aegir, the Ocean-king; but he wist not which way to go - whether across the North Sea towards Isenland, or whether along the narrow channel between Britain land and the main. While he paused, uncertain where to turn, he saw the pale-haired daughters of old Aegir, the white-veiled Waves, playing in the moonlight near the shore. Of them he asked the way to Aegir's hall.

"Seven days' journey westward," said they, "beyond the green Isle of Erin, is our father's hall. Seven days' journey northward, on the bleak Norwegian shore, is our father's hall. Seek it not."

And they stopped not once in their play, but rippled and danced on the shelving beach, or dashed with force against the shore.

"Where is your mother, Ran, the Queen of the Ocean?" asked Loki.

And they answered:

James Baldwin

"In the deep sea-caves
By the sounding shore,
In the dashing waves
When the wild storms roar,
In her cold green bowers
In the northern fiords,
She lurks and she glowers,
She grasps and she hoards,
And she spreads her strong net for her prey."

Loki waited to hear no more; but he sprang into the air, and the magic shoes carried him onwards over the water In search of the Ocean-queen. He had not gone far when his sharp eyes espied her, lurking near a rocky shore against which the breakers dashed with frightful fury. Half hidden in the deep dark water, she lay waiting and watching; and she spread her cunning net upon the waves, and reached out with her long greedy fingers to seize whatever booty might come near her.

When the wary queen saw Loki, she hastily drew in her net, and tried to hide herself in the shadows of an overhanging rock. But Loki called her by name, and said:

"Sister Ran, fear not! I am your friend Loki, whom once you served as a guest in Aegir's gold-lit halls."

Then the Ocean-queen came out into the bright moonlight, and welcomed Loki to her domain, and asked, "Why does Loki thus wander so far over the trackless waters?"

And Loki answered, "I have heard of the net which you spread upon the waves, and from which no creature once caught in its meshes can ever escape. I have found a salmon where the Rhine spring gushes from beneath the mountains, and a very cunning salmon he is, for no common skill can catch him. Come, I pray, with your wondrous net, and cast it into the stream where he lies. Do but take the wary fish for me, and you shall have more gold than you have taken in a year from the wrecks of stranded vessels."

"I dare not go," cried Ran. "A bound is set, beyond which I may not venture. If all the gold of earth were offered me, I could not go."

"Then lend me your net," entreated Loki. "Lend me your net, and I will bring it back tomorrow filled with gold."

"Much I would like your gold," answered Ran; "but I cannot lend my net. Should I do so, I might lose the richest prize that has ever come into my husband's kingdom. For three days, now, a gold-rigged ship, bearing a princely crew with rich armor and abundant wealth, has been sailing carelessly over these seas. Tomorrow I shall send my daughters and the bewitching mermaids to decoy the vessel among the rocks. And into my net the ship, and the brave warriors, and all their armor and gold, shall fall. A rich prize it will be. No: I cannot part with my net, even for a single hour."

But Loki knew the power of flattering words.

"Beautiful queen," said he, "there is no one on earth, nor even in Asgard, who can equal you in wisdom and foresight. Yet I promise you that, if you will but lend me your net until the morning dawns, the ship and the crew of which you speak shall be yours, and all their golden treasures shall deck your azure halls in the deep sea."

Then Ran carefully folded the net, and gave it to Loki.

"Remember your promise," was all that she said.

James Baldwin

"An Asa never forgets," he answered.

And he turned his face again towards Rhineland; and the magic shoes bore him aloft and carried him in a moment back to the ice mountain and the gorge and the infant river, which he had so lately left. The salmon still rested in his place, and had not moved during Loki's short absence.

Loki unfolded the net, and cast it into the stream. The cunning fish tried hard to avoid being caught in its meshes; but, dart which way he would, he met the skilfully woven cords, and these drew themselves around him, and held him fast. Then Loki pulled the net up out of the water, and grasped the helpless fish in his right hand. But, lo! as he held the struggling creature high in the air, it was no longer a fish, but the cunning dwarf Andvari.

"Thou King of the Elves," cried Loki, "thy cunning has not saved thee. Tell me, on thy life, where thy hidden treasures lie!"

The wise dwarf knew who it was that thus held him as in a vise; and he answered frankly, for it was his only hope of escape, "Turn over the stone upon which you stand. Beneath it you will find the treasure you seek."

Then Loki put his shoulder to the rock, and pushed with all his might. But it seemed as firm as the mountain, and would not be moved.

"Help us, thou cunning dwarf," he cried - "help us, and thou shalt have thy life!"

The dwarf put his shoulder to the rock, and it turned over as if by magic, and underneath was disclosed a wondrous chamber, whose walls shone brighter than the sun, and on whose floor lay treasures of gold and glittering gem stones such as no man had ever seen. And Loki, in great haste, seized upon the hoard, and placed it in the magic net which he had borrowed from the Ocean-queen. Then he came out of the chamber; and Andvari again put his shoulder to the rock which lay at the entrance, and it swung back noiselessly to its place.

"What is that upon thy finger?" suddenly cried Loki. "Wouldst keep back a part of the treasure? Give me the ring thou hast!"

But the dwarf shook his head, and made answer, "I have given thee all the riches that the elves of the mountain have gathered since the world began. This ring I cannot give thee, for without its help we shall never be able to gather more treasures together."

Loki grew very angry at these words of the dwarf; and he seized the ring, and tore it by force from Andvari's finger. It was a wondrous little piece of mechanism shaped like a serpent, coiled, with its tail in its mouth; and its scaly sides glittered with many a tiny diamond, and its ruby eyes shone with an evil light. When the dwarf knew that Loki really meant to rob him of the ring, he cursed it and all who should ever possess it, saying:

"May the ill-gotten treasure that you have seized to-night be your bane, and the bane of all to whom it may come, whether by fair means or by foul! And the ring which you have torn from my hand, may it entail upon the one who wears it sorrow and untold ills, the loss of friends, and a violent death!"

Loki was pleased with these words, and with the dark curses which the dwarf pronounced upon the gold; for he loved wrong-doing for wrong-doing's sake, and he knew

James Baldwin

that no curses could ever make his own life more cheerless than it always had been. So he thanked Andvari for his curses and his treasures; then, throwing the magic net upon his shoulder, he sprang again into the air, and was carried swiftly back to Hunaland; and, just before the dawn appeared in the east, he alighted at the door of the farmhouse where Odin and Hoenir still lay bound with thongs, and guarded by the watchful Fafnir and Regin.

Then the farmer, Hreidmar, brought the otter's skin, and spread it upon the ground; and, lo! it grew, and spread out on all sides, until it covered an acre of ground. And he cried out, "Fulfil now your promise! Cover every hair of this hide with gold or with precious stones. If you fail to do this, then your lives, by your own agreement, are forfeited, and we shall do with you as we list."

Odin took the magic net from Loki's shoulder; and, opening it, he poured the treasures of the mountain elves upon the otter skin. And Loki and Hoenir spread the yellow pieces carefully and evenly over every part of the furry hide. But, after every piece had been laid in its place, Hreidmar saw near the otter's mouth a single hair uncovered; and he declared, that unless this hair, too, were covered, the bargain would be unfulfilled, and the treasures and lives of his prisoners would be forfeited.

The Asas were filled with dismay; for not another piece of gold, and not another precious stone, could they find in the net, although they searched with the greatest care. At last Odin took from his bosom the ring which Loki had stolen from the dwarf; for he had been so highly pleased with its form and workmanship, that he had hidden it, hoping that it would not be needed to complete the payment of the ransom. And they laid the ring upon the uncovered hair; and now no portion of the otter's skin could be seen. And Fafnir and Regin, the ransom being paid, loosed the shackles of Odin and Hoenir, and bade the three huntsmen go on their way.

Odin and Hoenir at once shook off their human disguises, and, taking their own forms again, hastened with all speed home to Asgard. But Loki tarried a little while, and said to Hreidmar and his sons:

"By your greediness and falsehood you have won for yourselves the Curse of the Earth, which lies before you. It shall be your bane. It shall be the bane of everyone who holds it. It shall kindle strife between father and son, between brother and brother. It shall make you mean, selfish, beastly. It shall transform you into monsters. The noblest king among men folk shall feel its curse. Such is gold, and such it shall ever be to its worshippers. And the ring which you have gotten shall impart to its possessor its own nature. Grasping, snaky, cold, unfeeling, shall he live; and death through treachery shall be his doom."

Then he turned away, delighted that he had thus left the curse of Andvari with Hreidmar and his sons, and hastened north-ward toward the sea; for he wished to redeem the promise that he had made to the Ocean-queen, to bring back her magic net, and to decoy the richly laden ship into her clutches.

No sooner were the strange huntsmen well out of sight than Fafnir and Regin began to ask their father to divide the glittering hoard with them.

"By our strength and through our advice," said they, "this great store has come into your hands. Let us place it in three equal heaps, and then let each take his share and go his way."

At this the farmer waxed very angry; and he loudly

declared that he would keep all the treasure for himself, and that his sons should not have any portion of it whatever. So Fafnir and Regin, nursing their disappointment, went to the fields to watch their sheep; but their father sat down to guard his new-gotten treasure. He took in his hand the glittering serpent ring, and gazed into its cold ruby eyes; and, as he gazed, all his thoughts were fixed upon his gold; and there was no room in his heart for love toward his fellows, nor for deeds of kindness, nor for the worship of the All-Father. And behold, as he continued to look at the snaky ring, a dreadful change came over him. The warm red blood, which until that time had leaped through his veins, and given him life and strength and human feelings, became purple and cold and sluggish; and selfishness, like serpent's poison, took hold of his heart. Then, as he kept on gazing at the hoard which lay before him, he began to lose his human shape; his body lengthened into many scaly folds, and he coiled himself around his loved treasures, - the very likeness of the ring upon which he had looked so long.

When the day drew near its close, Fafnir came back from the fields with his herd of sheep, and thought to find his father guarding the treasure, as he had left him in the morning; but instead he saw a glittering snake, fast asleep, encircling the hoard like a huge scaly ring of gold. His first thought was that the monster had devoured his father; and, hastily drawing his sword, with one blow he severed the serpent's head from its body. And, while yet the creature writhed in the death agony, he gathered up the hoard, and fled with it beyond the hills of Hunaland, until on the seventh day he came to a barren heath far from the homes or men. There he placed the treasures in one glittering heap; and he clothed himself in a wondrous mail-coat of gold that was found among them, and he put on the Helmet of Dread, which had once been the terror of the mid-world, and the like of which no man had ever seen; and then he gazed with greedy eyes upon the fateful ring, until he, too, was changed into a cold and slimy reptile, - a monster dragon. He coiled himself about the hoard; and, with his restless eyes forever open, he gloated day after day upon his loved gold, and watched with ceaseless care that no one should come near to despoil him of it. This was ages and ages ago; and still he wallows among his treasures on the Glittering Heath, and guards as of yore the garnered wealth of Andvari.

[1]Regin, one of the last of the race of Dwarfs, was a master smith and by some said to be the teacher of Siegfried. The story is supposed to have been related to Siegfried in the dusky smithy of the dwarf.

James Baldwin

THE FORGING OF BALMUNG

While Siegfried was still a young lad, his father sent him to live with a smith called Mimer, whose smithy was among the hills not far from the great forest. For in those early times the work of the smith was looked upon as the most worthy of all trades, - a trade which the gods themselves were not ashamed to follow. And this smith Mimer was a wonderful master, - the wisest and most cunning that the world had ever seen. Men said that he was akin to the dwarf-folk who had ruled the earth in the early days, and who were learned in every lore, and skilled in every craft; and they said that he was so exceeding old that no one could remember the day when he came to dwell in the land of Siegfried's people. Some said, too, that he was the keeper of a wonderful well, or flowing spring, the waters of which imparted wisdom and far-seeing knowledge to all who drank of them.

To Mimer's school, then, where he would be taught to work skilfully and to think wisely, Siegfried was sent, to be in all respects like the other pupils there. A coarse blue blouse and heavy leggings and a leathern apron took the place of the costly clothing which he had worn in his father's dwelling. On his feet were awkward wooden sandals, and his head was covered with a wolfskin cap. The dainty bed, with its downy pillows, wherein every night his mother had been wont, with gentle care, to see him safely covered, was given up for a rude heap of straw in a corner of the smithy. And the rich food to which he had been used gave place to the coarsest and humblest fare. But the lad did not complain. The days which he passed in the smithy were mirthful and happy; and the sound of his hammer rang cheerfully, and the sparks from his forge flew briskly, from morning till night.

And a wonderful smith he became. No one could do more work than he, and none wrought with greater skill. The heaviest chains and the strongest bolts, for prison or for treasure house, were but as toys in his stout hands, so easily and quickly did he beat them into shape. Cunning also was he in work of the most delicate and brittle kind. Ornaments of gold and silver studded with the rarest jewels, were fashioned into beautiful forms by his deft fingers. And among all of Mimer's apprentices none learned the master's lore so readily, or gained the master's favor more.

One morning the master, Mimer, came to the smithy with a troubled look upon his face. It was clear that something had gone amiss; and what it was the apprentices soon learned from the smith himself. Never, until lately, had any one questioned Mimer's right to be called the foremost smith in all the world; but now a rival had come forward. An unknown upstart - one Amilias, a giant of Burgundy - had made a suit of armor, which, he boasted, no stroke of sword could dint, and no blow of spear could scratch; and he had sent a challenge to all other smiths, both in the Rhine country and elsewhere, to equal that piece of workmanship, or else acknowledge themselves his underlings and vassals. For many days had Mimer himself toiled, alone and vainly, trying to forge a sword whose edge the boasted armor of Amilias could not foil; and now, in despair, he came to ask the help of his pupils and apprentices.

"Who among you is skilful enough to forge such a

James Baldwin

sword?" he asked,

One after another, the pupils shook their heads. And the foreman of the apprentices said, "I have heard much about that wonderful armor, and its extreme hardness, and I doubt if any skill can make a sword with edge so sharp and true as to cut into it. The best that can be done is to try to make another war coat whose temper shall equal that of Amilias's armor."

Then the lad Siegfried quickly said, "I will make such a sword as you want, - a blade that no war coat can foil. Give me but leave to try!"

The other pupils laughed in scorn, but Mimer checked them. "You hear how this boy can talk: we will see what he can do. He is the king's son, and we know that he has uncommon talent. He shall make the sword; but if, upon trial, it fail, I will make him rue the day."

Then Siegfried went to his task. And for seven days and seven nights the sparks never stopped flying from his forge; and the ringing of his anvil, and the hissing of the hot metal as he tempered it, were heard continuously. On the eighth day the sword was fashioned, and Siegfried brought it to Mimer.

The smith felt the razor edge of the bright weapon, and said, "This seems, indeed, a fair fire edge. Let us make a trial of its keenness."

Then a thread of wool as light as thistle-down was thrown upon water, and, as it floated there, Mimer struck it with the sword. The glittering blade cleft the thread in twain, and the pieces floated undisturbed upon the surface of the liquid.

"Well done!" cried the delighted smith. "Never have I seen a keener edge. If its temper is as true as its sharpness would lead us to believe, it will indeed serve me well."

But Siegfried took the sword again, and broke it into many pieces; and for three days he welded it in a white-hot fire, and tempered it with milk and oatmeal. Then, in sight of the sneering apprentices, a light ball of fine-spun wool was cast upon the flowing water of the brook; and it was caught in the swift eddies of the stream, and whirled about until it met the bared blade of the sword, which was held in Siegfried's hands. And the ball was parted as easily and clean as the rippling water, and not the smallest thread was moved out of its place.

Then back to the smithy Siegfried went again; and his forge glowed with a brighter fire, and his hammer rang upon the anvil with a cheerier sound, than ever before. He suffered none to come near, and no one ever knew what witchery he used. But some of his fellow pupils afterwards told how, in the dusky twilight, they had seen a one-eyed man, long-bearded, and clad in a cloud-gray kirtle, and wearing a sky-blue hood, talking with Siegfried at the smithy door. And they said that the stranger's face was at once pleasant and fearful to look upon, and that his one eye shone in the gloaming like the evening star, and that, when he had placed in Siegfried's hands bright shards, like pieces of a broken sword, he faded suddenly from their sight, and was seen no more.

For seven weeks the lad wrought day and night at his forge; and then, pale and haggard, but with a pleased smile upon his face, he stood before Mimer, with the sword in his hands. "It is finished," he said. "Behold the glittering terror! - the blade Balmung. Let us try its edge and prove its temper once again, that so we may know whether you can place your trust in it."

James Baldwin

Mimer looked long at the ruddy hilt of the weapon, and at the mystic runes that were scored upon its sides, and at the keen edge, which looked like a ray of sunlight in the gathering gloom of the evening. But no word came from his lips, and his eyes were dim and dazed; and he seemed as one lost in thoughts of days long past and gone.

Siegfried raised the blade high over his head; and the gleaming edge flashed hither and thither, like the lightning's play when Thor rides over the storm clouds. Then suddenly it fell upon the master's anvil, and the solid block of iron was cleft in two; but the blade was no whit dulled by the stroke, and the line of light which marked the edge was brighter than before.

Then to the brook they went; and a great pack of wool, the fleeces of ten sheep, was brought, and thrown upon the swirling water. As the stream bore the bundle downwards, Mimer held the sword in its way. And the whole was divided as easily and as clean as the woollen ball or the slender woollen thread had been cleft before.

"Now, indeed," cried Mimer, "I no longer fear to meet that upstart, Amilias. If his war coat can withstand the stroke of such a sword as Balmung, then I shall not be ashamed to be his underling. But, if this good blade is what it seems to be, it will not fail me; and I, Mimer the Old, shall still be called the wisest and greatest of smiths."

He sent word at once to Amilias, in Burgundyland, to meet him on a day, and settle forever the question as to which of the two should be the master, and which the underling. And heralds proclaimed it in every town and dwelling. When the time which had been set drew near, Mimer, bearing the sword Balmung, and followed by all his pupils and apprentices, wended his way toward the place of meeting. Through the forest they went, and then along the banks of the sluggish river, for many a league, to the height of land which marked the line between Siegfried's country and the country of the Burgundians. It was in this place, midway between the shops of Mimer and Amilias, that the great trial of metal and of skill was to be made. And here were already gathered great numbers of people from the Lowlands and from Burgundy, anxiously waiting for the coming of the champions.

When everything was in readiness for the contest, Amilias, clad in his boasted war coat, went up to the top of the hill, and sat upon a rock, and waited for Mimer's coming. As he sat there, he looked, to the people below, like some great castle tower; for he was a giant in size, and his coat of mail was so huge that twenty men of common mould might have found shelter, or hidden themselves, within it. As the smith Mimer, so dwarfish in stature, tolled up the steep hillside, Amilias smiled to see him; for he felt no fear of the slender, gleaming blade that was to try the metal of his war coat. And already a shout or expectant triumph went up from the throats of the Burgundian hosts, so sure were they of their champion's success.

But Mimer's friends waited in breathless silence, hoping, and yet fearing. Only Siegfried's father, the king, whispered to his queen, and said, "Knowledge is stronger than brute force. The smallest dwarf who has drunk from the well of the Knowing One may safely meet the stoutest giant in battle."

When Mimer reached the top of the hill, Amilias folded his huge arms, and smiled again; for he felt that this contest was mere play for him, and that Mimer was already as good as beaten, and his thrall. The smith paused a moment to take breath, and as he stood by the side of his foe he looked to those below like a mere black speck close beside a steel-gray castle tower.

"Are you ready?" asked the smith.

"Ready," answered Amilias. "Strike!"

Mimer raised the blade in the air, and for a moment the lightning seemed to play around his head. The muscles on his short, brawny arms, stood out like ropes; and then Balmung, descending, cleft the air from right to left. The waiting lookers-on in the plain below thought to hear the noise of clashing steel; but they listened in vain, for no sound came to their ears, save a sharp hiss like that which red hot iron gives when plunged into a tank of cold water. The huge Amilias sat unmoved, with his arms still folded upon his breast; but the smile had faded from his face.

"How do you feel now?" asked Mimer in a half-mocking tone.

"Rather strangely, as if cold iron had touched me," faintly answered the giant.

"Shake thyself!" cried Mimer.

Amilias did so, and, lo! he fell in two halves; for the sword had cut sheer through the vaunted war coat, and cleft in twain the great body incased within. Down tumbled the giant's head and his still folded arms; and they rolled with thundering noise to the foot of the hill, and fell with a fearful splash into the deep waters of the river; and there, fathoms down, they may even now be seen, when the water is clear, lying like gray rocks among the sand and gravel below. The rest of the body, with the armor which incased it, still sat upright in its place; and to this day travellers sailing down the river are shown on moonlit evenings the luckless armor of Amilias on the high hilltop. In the dim, uncertain light, one easily fancies it to be the ivy-covered ruins of some old castle of feudal times.

The master, Mimer, sheathed his sword, and walked slowly down the hillside to the plain, where his friends welcomed him with cheers and shouts of joy. But the Burgundians, baffled, and feeling vexed, turned silently homeward, nor cast a single look back to the scene of their disappointment and their ill-fated champion's defeat.

Siegfried went again with the master and his fellows to the smoky smithy, to his roaring bellows and ringing anvil, and to his coarse fare, and rude, hard bed, and to a life of labor. And while all men praised Mimer and his knowing skill, and the fiery edge of the sunbeam blade, no one knew that it was the boy Siegfried who had wrought that piece of workmanship.

IDUN AND HER APPLES

THE STORY TOLD IN AEGIR'S HALL

Idun is Bragi's wife. Very handsome is she; but the beauty of her face is by no means greater than the goodness of her heart. Right attentive is she to every duty, and her words and thoughts are always worthy and wise. A long time ago the good Asa-folk who dwell in heaven-towering Asgard, knowing how trustworthy Idun was, gave into her keeping a treasure which they would not have placed in the hands of any other person. This treasure was a box of apples, and Idun kept the golden key safely fastened to her girdle. You ask me why these folk should prize a box of apples so highly? I will tell you.

Old age, you know, spares none, not even Odin and his Asa-folk. They all grow old and gray; and, if there were no cure for age, they would become feeble, and toothless and blind, deaf, tottering, and weak-minded. The apples which Idun guarded so carefully were the priceless boon of youth. Whenever the Asas felt old age coming on, they went to her, and she gave them of her fruit; and, when they had tasted, they grew young and strong and hand-some again. Once, however, they came near losing the apples, - or losing rather Idun and her golden key, without which no one could ever open the box.

In those early days Odin delighted to come down now and then from his high home above the clouds, and to wander, disguised, among the woods and mountains, and by the seashore, and in wild desert places. For nothing pleases him more than to commune with Nature as she is found in the loneliness of vast solitudes, or in the boisterous uproar of the elements. Once on a time he took with him his friends Hoenir and Loki; and they rambled many days among the icy cliffs and along the barren shores of the great frozen sea. In that country there was no game, and no fish were found in the cold waters; and the three wanderers, as they had brought no food with them, became very hungry. Late in the afternoon of the seventh day, they reached some pasture lands belonging to the giant Hymer, and saw a herd of the giants cattle browsing upon the short grass which grew in the sheltered nooks among the hills.

"Ah!" cried Loki; "after fasting for a week we shall now have food in abundance. Let us kill and eat."

So saying, he hurled a sharp stone at the fattest of Hymer's cows, and killed her; and the three quickly dressed the choicest pieces of flesh for their supper. Then Loki gathered twigs and dry grass, and kindled a blazing fire; Hoenir filled the pot with water from melted ice; and Odin threw into it the bits of tender meat. But, make the fire as hot as they would, the water would not boil, and the flesh would not cook.

All night long the supperless three sat hungry around the fire; and, every time they peeped into the kettle, the meat was as raw and gustless as before. Morning came, but no breakfast. And all day long Loki kept stirring the fire, and Odin and Hoenir waited hopefully but impatiently. When the sun again went down, the flesh was still uncooked, and their supper seemed no nearer ready than it was the night before. As they were about yielding to despair, they heard a noise overhead; and, looking up, they saw a huge gray eagle sitting on the dead branch of an oak.

"Ha, ha!" cried the bird. "You are pretty fellows indeed! To sit hungry by the fire a night and a day, rather than eat raw flesh, becomes you well. Do but give me my share of it as it is, and I warrant you the rest shall boil, and you shall have a fat supper."

"Agreed," answered Loki eagerly. "Come down and get your share."

The eagle waited for no second asking. Down he swooped right over the blazing fire, and snatched not only the eagle's share, but also what the Lybians call the lion's share; that is, he grasped in his strong talons the kettle, with all the meat in it, and, flapping his huge wings, slowly rose into the air, carrying his booty with him. The three Asas were astonished. Loki was filled with anger. He seized a long pole, upon the end of which a sharp hook was fixed, and struck at the treacherous bird. The hook stuck fast in the eagle's back, and Loki could not loose his hold of the other end of the pole. The great bird soared high above the tree-tops, and over the hills, and carried the astonished mischief-maker with him.

But it was no eagle. It was no bird that had thus outwitted the hungry Asas: it was the giant Old Winter, clothed in his eagle plumage. Over the lonely woods, and the snow-crowned mountains, and the frozen sea, he flew, dragging the helpless Loki through tree-tops, and over jagged rocks, scratching and bruising his body, and almost tearing his arms from his shoulders. At last he alighted on the craggy top of an iceberg, where the storm winds shrieked, and the air was filled with driving snow. As soon as Loki could speak, he begged the cunning giant to carry him back to his comrades, - Odin and Hoenir.

"On one condition only will I carry you back," answered Old Winter. "Swear to me that you will betray into my hands Dame Idun and her golden key."

Loki asked no questions, but gladly gave the oath; and the giant flew back with him across the sea, and dropped him, torn and bleeding and lame, by the side of the fire, where Odin and Hoenir still lingered. And the three made all haste to leave that cheerless place, and returned to Odin's glad home in Asgard.

Some weeks after this, Loki, the Prince of Mischief-makers, went to Bragi's house to see Idun. He found her busied with her household cares, not thinking of a visit from anyone.

"I have come, good dame," said he, "to taste your apples again; for I feel old age coming on apace."

Idun was astonished.

"You are not looking old," she answered. "There is not a single gray hair upon your head, and not a wrinkle on your brow. If it were not for that scar upon your cheek, and the arm which you carry in a sling, you would look as stout and as well as I have ever seen you. Besides, I remember that it was only a year ago when you last tasted of my fruit. Is it possible that a single winter should make you old?"

"A single winter has made me very lame and feeble at least," said Loki. "I have been scarcely able to walk about since my return from the North. Another winter without a taste of your apples will be the death of me."

Then the kind-hearted Idun, when she saw that Loki was really lame, went to the box, and opened it with her golden key, and gave him one of the precious apples to taste. He took the fruit in his hand, bit it, and gave it back to the good dame. She put it in its place again, closed the lid, and locked it with her usual care.

"Your apples are not so good as they used to be," said Loki, making a very wry face. "Why don't you fill your box with fresh fruit?"

Idun was amazed. Her apples were supposed to be always fresh, - fresher by far than any that grow nowadays. None of the Asas had ever before complained about them; and she told Loki so.

"Very well," said he. "I see you do not believe me, and that you mean to feed us on your sour, withered apples, when we might as well have golden fruit. If you were not so bent on having your own way, I could tell you where you might fill your box with the choicest of apples, such as Odin loves. I saw them in the forest over yonder, hanging ripe on the trees. But women will always have their own way; and you must have yours, even though you do feed us on withered apples."

So saying, and without waiting to hear an answer, he limped out at the door, and was soon gone from sight.

Idun thought long and anxiously upon the words which Loki had spoken; and, the more she thought, the more she felt troubled. If her husband, the wise Bragi, had been at home, what would she not have given? He would have understood the mischief-maker's cunning. But he had gone on a long journey to the South, singing in Nature's choir and painting Nature's landscapes, and she would not see him again until the return of spring. At length she opened the box, and looked at the fruit. The apples were certainly fair and round: she could not see a wrinkle or a blemish on any of them; their color was the same golden-red, - like the sky at dawn of a summer's day; yet she thought there must be something wrong about them. She took up one of the apples, and tasted it. She fancied that it really was sour, and she hastily put it back, and locked the box again.

"He said that he had seen better apples than these growing in the woods," said she to herself. "I half believe that he told the truth, although everybody knows that he is not always trust-worthy. I think I shall go to the forest and see for myself, at any rate."

So she donned her cloak and hood, and, with a basket on her arm, left the house, and walked rapidly away, along the road which led to the forest. It was much farther than she had thought, and the sun was almost down when she reached the edge of the wood. But no apple trees were there. Tall oaks stretched their bare arms up toward the sky, as if praying for help. There were thorn trees and brambles everywhere; but there was no fruit, neither were there any flowers, nor even green leaves. The Frost-giants had been there.

Idun was about to turn her footsteps homeward, when she heard a wild shriek in the tree-tops over her head; and, before she could look up, she felt herself seized in the eagle talons of Old Winter. Struggle as she would, she could not free herself. High up, over wood and stream, the giant carried her; and then he flew swiftly away with her, toward his home in the chill Northland; and, when morning came, poor Idun found herself in an ice-walled castle in the cheerless country of the giants. But she was glad to know that the precious box was safely locked at home, and that the golden key was still at her girdle.

Time passed; and I fear that Idun would have been

James Baldwin

forgotten by all, save her husband Bragi, had not the Asas begun to feel the need of her apples. Day after day they came to Idun's house, hoping to find the good dame and her golden key at home; and each day they went away some hours older than when they had come. No one had seen the missing Idun since the day when Loki had visited her, and none could guess what had become of her. The heads of all the folk grew white with age; deep furrows were ploughed in their faces; their eyes grew dim, and their hearing failed; their hands trembled; their limbs became palsied; their feet tottered; and all feared that Old Age would bring Death in his train.

Then Bragi and Thor questioned Loki very sharply; and when he felt that he, too, was growing old and feeble, he regretted the mischief he had done, and told them how he had decoyed Idun into Old Winter's clutches. The Asas were very angry; and Thor threatened to crush Loki with his hammer, if he did not at once bring Idun safe home again.

So Loki borrowed the falcon plumage of Freyja, the queen of love, and with it flew to the country of the giants. When he reached Old Winter's castle, he found the good dame Idun shut up in the prison tower and bound with fetters of ice; but the giant himself was on the frozen sea, herding Old Hymer's cows, the cold icebergs. Loki quickly broke the bonds that held Idun, and led her out of her prison house; and then he shut her up in a magic nut-shell which he held between his claws, and flew with the speed of the wind back toward the Southland and the home of the Asas. But Old Winter coming home, and learning what had been done, donned his eagle plumage and followed swiftly in pursuit.

Bragi and Thor, anxiously gazing into the sky, saw Loki, in Freyja's falcon plumage, speeding homeward, with the nut-shell in his talons, and Old Winter, in his eagle plumage, dashing after in sharp pursuit. Quickly they gathered chips and slender twigs, and placed them high upon the castle wall; and, when Loki with his precious burden had flown past, they touched fire to the dry heap, and the flames blazed up to the sky, and caught Old Winter's plumage, as, close behind the falcon, he blindly pressed. And his wings were scorched in the flames; and he fell helpless to the ground, and was slain within the castle gates. Loki slackened his speed; and, when he reached Bragi's house, he dropped the nut-shell softly before the door. As it touched the ground, it gently opened, and Idun, radiant with smiles, and clothed in gay attire, stepped forth, and greeted her husband and his waiting friends. The heavenly music of Bragi's long-silent harp welcomed her home; and she took the golden key from her girdle, and unlocked the box, and gave of her apples to the aged company; and, when they had tasted, their youth was renewed.

It is thus with the seasons and their varied changes. The gifts of Spring are youth and jollity, and renewed strength; and the music or air and water and all things, living and lifeless, follow in her train. The desolating Winter plots to steal her from the earth, and the Summer-heat deserts and betrays her. Then the music of Nature is hushed, and all creatures pine in sorrow for her absence, and the world seems dying of white Old Age. But at length the Summer-heat repents, and frees her from her prison house; the icy fetters with which Old Winter bound her are melted in the beams of the returning sun, and the earth is young again.

THE DOOM OF THE MISCHIEF-MAKER.

You have heard of the feast that old Aegir once made for the Asa-folk in his gold-lit dwelling in the deep sea, and how the feast was hindered, through the loss of his great brewing kettle, until Thor had obtained a still larger vessel from Hymer the giant. It is very likely that the thief who stole King Aegir's kettle was none other than Loki the Mischief-maker; but, if this was so, he was not long unpunished for his meanness.

There was great joy in the Ocean-king's hall, when at last the banquet was ready, and the foaming mead began to pass itself around to the guests. But Thor, who had done so much to help matters along, could not stay to the merry-making: for he had heard that the Storm-giants were marshalling their forces for a raid upon some unguarded corner of the mid-world; and so, grasping his hammer, he bade his kind host good-by, and leaped into his iron car.

"Business always before pleasure!" he cried, as he hastened away at a wonderful rate through the air.

In old Aegir's hall glad music resounded on every side; and the gleeful Waves danced merrily as the Asa-folk sat around the festal board, and partook of the Ocean-king's good fare. Aegir's two thralls, the faithful Funfeng and the trusty Elder, waited upon the guests and carefully supplied their wants. Never in all the world had two more thoughtful servants been seen; and every one spoke in praise of their quickness, and their skill, and their ready obedience.

Then Loki, unable to keep his hands from mischief, waxed very angry, because every one seemed happy and free from trouble, and no one noticed or cared for him. So, while good Funfeng was serving him to meat, he struck the faithful thrall with a carving-knife, and killed him. Then arose a great uproar in the Ocean-king's feast hall. The Asa-folk rose up from the table, and drove the Mischief-maker out from among them; and in their wrath they chased him across the waters, and forced him to hide in the thick greenwood. After this they went back to Aegir's hall, and sat down again to the feast. But they had scarcely begun to eat, when Loki came quietly out of his hiding place, and stole slyly around to Aegir's kitchen, where he found Elder, the other thrall, grieving sadly because of his brother's death.

"I hear a great chattering and clattering over there in the feast hall," said Loki. "The greedy, silly Asa-folk seem to be very busy indeed, both with their teeth and their tongues. Tell me, now, good Elder, what they talk about while they sit over their meat."

"They talk of noble deeds," answered Elder. "They speak of gallant heroes, and brave men, and fair women, and strong hearts, and willing hands, and gentle manners, and kind friends. And for all these they have words of praise and songs of beauty; but none of them speak well of Loki, the thief and the vile traitor."

"Ah!" said Loki wrathfully, twisting himself into a dozen different shapes, "no one could ask so great a kindness from such folk. I must go into the feast hall, and take a look at this fine company, and listen to their noisy merry-making. I have a fine scolding laid up for those good fellows; and, unless they are careful with their tongues, they will find many hard words mixed with their mead."

Then he went boldly into the great hall, and stood up before the wonder-stricken guests at the table. When the Asa-folk saw who it was that had darkened the doorway, and was now in their midst, a painful silence fell upon them, and all their merriment was at an end. And Loki stretched himself up to his full height, and said to them:

"Hungry and thirsty came I to Aegir's gold-lit hall. Long and rough was the road I trod, and wearisome was the way. Will no one bid me welcome? Will none give me a seat at the feast? Will none offer me a drink of the precious mead? Why are you all so dumb? Why so sulky and stiff-necked, when your best friend stands before you? Give me a seat among you, - yes, one of the high seats, - or else drive me from your hall! In either case, the world will never forget me. I am Loki."

Then one among the Asa-folk spoke up, and said, "Let him sit with us. He is mad; and when he slew Funfeng, he was not in his right mind. He is not answerable for his rash act."

But Bragi the Wise, who sat on the innermost seat, arose, and said, "Nay, we will not give him a seat among us. Nevermore shall he feast or sup with us, or share our good-fellowship. Thieves and murderers we know, and we will shun them."

This speech enraged Loki all the more; and he spared not vile words, but heaped abuse without stint upon all the folk before him. By main force he seized hold of the silent Vidar, who had come from the forest solitudes to be present at the feast, and dragged him away from the table, and seated himself in his place. Then, as he quaffed the foaming mead, he flung out taunts and jeers and hard words to all who sat around, but chiefly to Bragi the Wise and Sif, the beautiful wife of Thor.

Suddenly a great tumult was heard outside. The mountains shook and trembled; the bottom of the sea seemed moved; and the waves, affrighted and angry, rushed hither and thither in confusion. All the guests looked up in eager expectation, and some of them fled in alarm from the hall. Then the mighty Thor strode in at the door, and up to the table, swinging his hammer, and casting wrathful glances at the Mischief-maker. Loki trembled; he dropped his goblet, and sank down upon his knees before the terrible Asa.

"I yield me!" he cried. "Spare my life, I pray you, and I will be your thrall forever!"

"I want no such thrall," answered Thor. "And I spare your life on one condition only, - that you go at once from hence, and nevermore presume to come into the company of Asa-folk."

"I promise all that you ask," said Loki, trembling more than ever. "Let me go."

Thor stepped aside; and the frightened culprit fled from the hall, and was soon out of sight. The feast was broken up. The Asas bade Aegir a kind farewell, and favoring winds wafted them swiftly home to Asgard.

Loki fled to the dark mountain gorges of Mist Land, and sought for a while to hide himself from the sight of both gods and men. In a deep ravine by the side of a roaring torrent, he built himself a house of iron and stone, and

James Baldwin

placed a door on each of its four sides, so that he could see whatever passed around him. There, for many winters, he lived in lonely solitude, planning with himself how he might baffle his enemies and regain his old place in Asgard. Now and then he slipped slyly away from his hiding-place, and wrought much mischief for a time among the abodes of men. But when Thor heard of his evil-doings, and sought to catch him, and punish him for his evil deeds, he was nowhere to be found. At last the Asa-folk determined, that, if he could ever be captured, the safety of the world required that he should be bound hand and foot, and kept forever in prison.

Loki often amused himself in his mountain home by taking upon him his favorite form of a salmon and lying listlessly beneath the waters of the great Fanander Cataract, which fell from the shelving rocks a thousand feet above him. One day while thus lying, he bethought himself of former days, when he walked the glad young earth in company with great Odin. And among other things he remembered how he had once borrowed the magic net of Ran, the Ocean-queen, and had caught with it the dwarf Andvari, disguised, as he himself now was, in the form of a slippery salmon.

"I will make me such a net!" he cried. "I will make it strong and good; and I, too, will fish for men."

So he took again his proper shape, and went back to his cheerless home in the ravine. There he gathered flax and wool and long hemp, and spun yarn and strong cords, and wove them into meshes, after the pattern of Queen Ran's magic net; for men had not, at that time, learned how to make or use nets for fishing. And the first fisherman who caught fish in that way is said to have taken-Loki's net as a model.

Odin sat, on the morrow, in his high hall at Asgard, and looked out over all the world, even to the uttermost corners. With his sharp eye he saw what men-folk were everywhere doing. When his gaze rested upon the dark line which marked the mountain land of the Mist Country, he started up in quick surprise, and cried out:

"Who is that who sits by the Fanander Falls, and ties strong cords together?"

But none of those who stood around could tell, for their eyes were not strong enough and clear enough to see so far.

"Bring Heimdal!" then cried Odin.

Now, Heimdal the White dwells among the blue mountains where the rainbow spans the space betwixt heaven and earth. He is the son of Odin, golden-toothed, pure-faced, and clean-hearted; and he ever keeps watch and ward over the mid-world and the homes of frail men-folk, lest the giants shall break in, and destroy and slay. He rides upon a shining steed named Goldtop; and he holds in his hand a horn with which, in the last twilight, he shall summon the world to battle with the sons of Loki. This watchful guardian of the mid-world is as wakeful as the birds. And his hearing is so keen, that no sound on earth escapes him, - not even that of the rippling waves upon the seashore, nor of the quiet sprouting of the grass in the meadows, nor even of the growth of the soft wool on the backs of the sheep. His eyesight, too, is wondrous clear and sharp; for he can see by night as well as by day, and the smallest thing, although a hundred leagues away, cannot be hidden from him.

To Heimdal, then, the heralds hastened, bearing the words which Odin had spoken, and the watchful warder of the

James Baldwin

mid-world came at once to the call of the All-Father.

"Turn your eyes to the sombre mountains that guard the shadowy Mist Land from the sea," said Odin. "Now look far down into the rocky gorge in which the Fanander Cataract pours, and tell me what you see."

Heimdal did as he was bidden.

"I see a shape," said he, "sitting by the torrent's side. It is Loki's shape, and he seems strangely busy with strong strings and cords."

"Call all our folk together!" commanded Odin. "The wily Mischief-maker plots our hurt. He must be driven from his hiding place, and put where he can do no further harm."

Great stir was there then in Asgard. Every one hastened to answer Odin's call, and to join in the quest for the Mischief-maker. Thor came on foot, with his hammer tightly grasped in his hands, and lightning flashing from beneath his red brows. Tyr, the one-handed, came with his sword. Then followed Bragi the Wise, with his harp and his sage counsels; then Hermod the Nimble, with his quick wit and ready hands; and lastly, a great company of elves and wood-sprites and trolls. Then a whirlwind caught them up in its swirling arms, and carried them through the air, over the hilltops and the countryside, and the meadows and the mountains, and set them down in the gorge of the Fanander Force.

But Loki was not caught napping. His wakeful ears had heard the tumult in the air, and he guessed who it was that was coming. He threw the net, which he had just finished, into the fire, and jumped quickly into the swift torrent, where, changing himself into a salmon, he lay hidden beneath the foaming water.

When the eager Asa-folk reached Loki's dwelling, they found that he whom they sought had fled; and although they searched high and low, among the rocks and the caves and the snowy crags, they could see no signs of the cunning fugitive. Then they went back to his house again to consult what next to do. And, while standing by the hearth, Kwaser, a sharp-sighted elf, whose eyes were quicker than the sunbeam, saw the white ashes of the burned net lying undisturbed in the still hot embers, the woven meshes unbroken and whole.

"See what the cunning fellow has been making!" cried the elf. "It must have been a trap for catching fish."

"Or rather for catching men," said Bragi; "for it is strangely like the Sea-queen's net."

"In that case," said Hermod the Nimble, "he has made a trap for himself; for, no doubt, he has changed himself, as is his wont, to a slippery salmon, and lies at this moment hidden beneath the Fanander torrent. Here are plenty of cords of flax and hemp and wool, with which he intended to make other nets. Let us take them, and weave one like the pattern which lies there in the embers; and then, if I mistake not, we shall catch the too cunning fellow."

All saw the wisdom of these words, and all set quickly to work. In a short time they had made a net strong and large, and full of fine meshes, like the model among the coals. Then they threw it into the roaring stream, Thor holding to one end, and all the other folk pulling it the other. With great toil, they dragged it forward, against the current, even to the foot of the waterfall. But the cunning Loki crept close down between two sharp stones, and lay there quietly while the net passed harmlessly over him.

"Let us try again!" cried Thor. "I am sure that something besides dead rocks lies at the bottom of the stream."

So they hung heavy weights to the net, and began to drag it again, this time going down stream. Loki looked out from his hiding place, and saw that he would not be able to escape now by lying between the rocks, and that his only chance for safety was either to leap over the net, and hide himself behind the rushing cataract itself, or to swim with the current out to the sea. But the way to the sea was long, and there were many shallow places; and Loki had doubts as to how old Aegir would receive him in his kingdom. He feared greatly to undertake so dangerous and uncertain a course. So, turning upon his foes, and calling up all his strength, he made a tremendous leap high into the air and clean over the net. But Thor was too quick for him. As he fell toward the water, the Thunderer quickly threw out his hand, and caught the slippery salmon, holding him firmly by the tail.

When Loki found that he was surely caught, and could not by any means escape, he took again his proper shape. Fiercely did he struggle with mighty Thor, and bitter were the curses which he poured down upon his enemies. But he could not get free. Into the deep, dark cavern, beneath the smoking mountain, where daylight never comes, nor the warmth of the sun, nor the sound of Nature's music, the fallen Mischief-maker was carried. The Asas bound him firmly to the sharp rocks, with his face turned upwards toward the dripping roof; for they said that nevermore, until the last dread twilight, should he be free to vex the world with his wickedness. Skade, the giant daughter of Old Winter, took a hideous snake, and hung it up above Loki, so that its venom would drop into his upturned face. But Sigyn, the loving wife of the suffering wretch, left her home in the pleasant halls of Asgard, and came to his horrible prison house to soothe and comfort him; and evermore she holds a basin above his head, and catches in it the poisonous drops as they fall. When the basin is filled, and she turns to empty it in the tar-black river that flows through that home of horrors, the terrible venom falls upon his unprotected face, and Loki writhes and shrieks in fearful agony, until the earth around him shakes and trembles, and the mountains spit forth fire, and fumes of sulphur smoke.

And there the Mischief-maker, the spirit of evil, shall lie in torment until the last great day and the dread twilight of all mid-world things.

James Baldwin

THE HUNT IN THE WOOD OF PUELLE

RELATED BY THE MINSTREL OF LORRAINE[1]

Charles the Hammer was dead, and his young son Pepin was king of France. Bego of Belin was his dearest friend, and to him he had given all Gascony in fief. You would have far to go to find the peer of the valiant Bego. None of King Pepin's nobles dared gainsay him. Rude in speech and rough in war, though he was, he was a true knight, gentle and loving to his friends, very tender to his wife and children, kind to his vassals, just and upright in all his doings. The very flower of knighthood was Bego.

Bitter feuds had there been between the family of Bego and that of Fromont of Bordeaux. Long time had these quarrels continued, and on both sides much blood had been spilled. But now there had been peace between them for ten years and more, and the old hatred was being forgotten.

One day Bego sat in his lordly castle at Belin; and beside him was his wife, the fair Beatrice. In all France there was not a happier man. From the windows the duke looked out upon his broad lands and the rich farms of his tenants. As far as a bird could fly in a day, all was his; and his vassals and serving-men were numbered by the tens of thousands. "What more," thought Bego, "could the heart of man wish or pray for?"

His two young sons came bounding into the hall, - Gerin, the elder born, fair-haired and tall, brave and gentle as his father; and Hernaudin, the younger, a child of six summers, his mother's pet, and the joy of the household. With them were six other lads, sons of noblemen; and all together laughed and played, and had their boyish pleasure.

When the duke saw them, he remembered his own boyhood days and the companions who had shared his sports, and he sighed. The fair Beatrice heard him, and she said, "My lord, what ails you, that you are so thoughtful to-day? Why should a rich duke like you sigh and seem sad? Great plenty of gold and silver have you in your coffers; you have enough of the vair and the gray,[2] of hawks on their perches, of mules and palfreys and war steeds; you have overcome all your foes, and none dare rise up against you. All within six days' journey are your vassals. What more would you desire to make you happy?"

"Sweet lady," answered Bego, "you have spoken truly. I am rich, as the world goes; but my wealth is not happiness. True wealth is not of money, of the vair and the gray, of mules, or of horses. It is of kinsfolk and friends. The heart of a man is worth more than all the gold of a country. Had it not been for my friends, I would have been put to shame long ago. The king has given me this fief, far from my boyhood's home, where I see but few of my old comrades and helpers. I have not seen my brother Garin, the Lorrainer, these seven years, and my heart yearns to behold him. Now, methinks, I will go to him, and I will see his son, the child Girbert, whom I have never seen."

The Lady Beatrice said not a word, but the tears began to well up sadly in her eyes.

"In the wood of Puelle," said Bego, after a pause, "there is said to be a wild boar, the largest and fiercest ever seen. He outruns the fleetest horses. No man can slay him. Methinks, that if it please God, and I live, I will hunt in that wood, and I will carry the head of the great beast to my brother the Lorrainer."

Then Beatrice, forcing back her tears, spoke:

"Sir," said she, "what is it thou sayest? The wood of Puelle is in the march of Fromont the chief, and he owes thee a great grudge. He would be too glad to do thee harm. I pray thee do not undertake this hunt. My heart tells me, - I will not hide the truth from thee, - my heart tells me, that if thou goest thither thou shalt never come back alive."

But the duke laughed at her fears; and the more she tried to dissuade him, the more he set his mind on seeing his brother the Lorrainer, and on carrying to him the head of the great wild boar of Puelle. Neither prayers nor tears could turn him from his purpose. All the gold in the world, he said, would not tempt him to give up the adventure.

So on the morrow morning, before the sun had fairly risen, Bego made ready to go. As this was no warlike enterprise, he dressed himself in the richest garb of knightly hero, - with mantle of ermine, and spurs of gold. With him he took three dozen huntsmen, all skilled in the lore of the woods, and ten packs of hunting hounds. He had, also, ten horses loaded with gold and silver and costly presents, and more than a score of squires and serving-men. Tenderly he bade fair Beatrice and his two young sons good-by. Ah, what grief! Never was he to see them more.

Going by way of Orleans, Bego stopped a day with his sister, the lovely Helois. Three days he tarried at Paris, the honored guest of the king and queen. Then pushing on to Valencie-nnes, which was on the borders of the great forest, he took up lodging with a rich burgher called Berenger the Gray.

"Thou hast many foes in these parts," said the burgher, "and thou wouldst do well to ware of them."

Bego only laughed at the warning. "Didst thou ever know a Gascon to shun danger?" he asked. "I have heard of the famed wild boar of Puelle, and I mean to hunt him in this wood, and slay him. Neither friends nor foes shall hinder me."

On the morrow Berenger led the duke and his party into the wood, and showed them the lair of the beast. Out rushed the monster upon his foes; then swiftly he fled, crashing through brush and brake, keeping well out of the reach of the huntsmen, turning every now and then to rend some too venturesome hound. For fifteen leagues across the country he led the chase. One by one the huntsmen lost sight of him. Toward evening a cold rain came up; and they turned, and rode back toward Valenciennes. They had not seen the duke since noon. They supposed that he had gone back with Berenger. But Bego was still riding through the forest in close pursuit of the wild boar. Only three hounds kept him company.

The boar was well-nigh wearied out, and the duke knew that he could not go much farther. He rode up close behind him; and the fierce animal, his mouth foaming with rage, turned furiously upon him. But the duke, with a well-aimed thrust of his sword, pierced the great beast through his heart.

By this time, night was falling. The duke knew that he was very far from any town or castle, but he hoped that some of his men might be within call. He took his horn, and blew it twice full loudly. But his huntsmen were now riding into Valenciennes; nor did they think that they had left their master behind them in the wood. With his flint the duke kindled a fire; beneath an aspen tree, and made ready to spend the night near the place where the slain wild boar lay.

The forester who kept the wood heard the sound of Bego's horn, and saw the light of the fire gleaming through the trees. Cautiously he drew nearer. He was surprised to see a knight so richly clad, with his silken hose and his golden spurs, his ivory horn hanging from his neck by a blue ribbon. He noticed the great sword that hung at Bego's side. It was the fairest and fearfulest weapon he had ever seen. He hastened as fast as he could ride to Lens, where Duke Fromont dwelt; but he spoke not a word to Fromont. He took the steward of the castle aside, and told him of what he had seen in the wood.

"He is no common huntsman," said the forester; "and you should see how richly clad he is. No king was ever arrayed more gorgeously while hunting. And his horse - I never saw a better."

"But what is all this to me?" asked the steward. "If he is trespassing in the forest, it is your duty to bring him before the duke."

"Ah! it is hard for you to understand," answered the forester. "Methinks that if our master had the boar, the sword, and the horn, he would let me keep the clothing, and you the horse, and would trouble us with but few questions."

"Thou art indeed wise," answered the steward. And he at once called six men, whom he knew he could trust to any evil deed, and told them to go with the forester.

"And, if you find any man trespassing in Duke Fromont's wood, spare him not," he added.

In the morning the ruffians came to the place where Duke Bego had spent the night. They found him sitting not far from the great beast which he had slain, while his horse stood before him and neighed with impatience and struck his hoofs upon the ground. They asked him who gave him leave to hunt in the wood of Puelle.

"I ask no man's leave to hunt where it pleases me," he answered.

They told him then that the lordship of the wood was with Fromont and that he must go with them, as their prisoner, to Lens.

"Very well," said Bego. "I will go with you. If I have done aught of wrong to Fromont the old, I am willing to make it right with him. My brother Garin, the Lorrainer, and King Pepin, will go my surety."

Then, looking around upon the villainous faces of the men who had come to make prisoner of him, he bethought himself for a moment.

"No, no!" he cried. "Never will I yield me to six such rascals. Before I die, I will sell myself full dear. Yesterday six and thirty knights were with me, and master huntsmen, skilled in all the lore of the wood. Noble men were they all; for not one of them but held in fief some town or castle or rich countryside. They will join me ere long."

"He speaks thus, either to excuse himself or to frighten us," said one of the men; and he went boldly forward, and tried to snatch the horn from Bego's neck. The duke raised his fist, and knocked him senseless to the ground.

"Never shall ye take horn from count's neck!" he cried.

Then all set upon him at once, hoping that by their numbers they might overpower him. But Bego drew his sword, and struck valiantly to the right and to the left of him. Three of the villains were slain outright; and the rest took to their heels and fled, glad to escape such fury.

And now all might have been well with Duke Bego. But a churl, armed with a bow, and arrows of steel, was hidden among the trees. When he saw his fellows put to flight, he drew a great steel bolt and aimed it at the duke. Swiftly sped the arrow toward the noble targe: too truly was it aimed. The duke's sword fell from his hands: the master-vein of his heart had been cut in twain. He lifted his hands toward heaven, and prayed: -

"Almighty Father, who always wert and art, have pity on my soul. - Ah, Beatrice! thou sweet, gentle wife, never more shalt thou see me under heaven. - Fair brother Garin of Lorraine, never shall I be with thee to serve thee. - My two noble boys, if I had lived, you should have been the worthiest of knights: now, may Heaven defend you!"

After a while the churl and the three villains came near him, and found him dead. It was no common huntsman whom they had killed, but a good knight, - the loyalest and the best that ever God's sun shone upon. They took the sword and the horn and the good steed; they loaded the boar upon a horse; and all returned to Lens. But they left Bego in the forest, and with him his three dogs, who sat around him, and howled most mournfully, as if they knew they had lost their best friend.

The men carried the great boar into the castle of Lens, and threw it down upon the kitchen hearth. A wonderful beast he was: his sharp, curved tusks stuck out full a foot from his mouth. The serving-men and the squires crowded around to see the huge animal; then, as the news was told through the castle, many fair ladies and knights, and the priests from the chapel, came in to view the sight. Old Duke Fromont heard the uproar, and came in slippers and gown to ask what it all meant.

"Whence came this boar, this ivory horn, this sword?" he inquired. "This horn never belonged to a mere huntsman. It looks like the wondrous horn that King Charles the Hammer had in the days of my father. There is but one knight now living that can blow it; and he is far away in Gascony. Tell me where you got these things."

Then the forester told him all that had happened in the wood, coloring the story, of course, so as to excuse himself from wrong-doing.

"And left ye the slain man in the wood?" asked the old duke. "A more shameful sin I have never known than to leave him there for the wolves to eat. Go ye back at once, and fetch him hither. To-night he shall be watched in the chapel, and to-morrow he shall be buried with all due honor. Men should have pity of one another."

The body of the noble Duke Bego was brought, and laid upon a table in the great hall. His dogs were still with him, howling pitifully, and licking his face. Knights and noblemen came in to see him.

"A gentle man this was," said they; "for even his dogs loved him."

"Shame on the rascals who slew him!" said others. "No freeman would have touched so noble a knight."

Old Duke Fromont came in. He started back at sight of him who lay there lifeless. Well he knew Duke Bego, by a scar that he himself had given him at the battle of St. Quentin ten years before. He fell fainting into the arms of his knights. Then afterward he upbraided his men for their dastardly deed, and bewailed their wicked folly.

"This is no poaching huntsman whom you have slain," said he, "but a most worthy knight, - the kindest, the best taught, that ever wore spurs. And ye have dragged me this day into such a war that I shall not be out of it so long as I live. I shall see my lands overrun and wasted, my great castles thrown down and destroyed, and my people distressed and slain; and as for myself I shall have to die - and all this for a fault which is none of mine, and for a deed which I have neither wished nor sanctioned."

And the words of Duke Fromont were true. The death of Bego of Belin was fearfully avenged by his brother the Lorrainer and by his young sons Gerin and Hernaud. Never was realm so impoverished as was Fromont's dukedom. The Lorrainers and the Gascons overran and laid waste the whole country. A pilgrim might go six days' journey without finding bread, or meat, or wine. The crucifixes lay prone upon the ground; the grass grew upon the altars; and no man stopped to plead with his neighbor. Where had been fields and houses, and fair towns and lordly castles, now there was naught but woods and underbrush and thorns. And old Duke Fromont, thus ruined through no fault of his own, bewailed his misfortunes, and said to his friends, "I have not land enough to rest upon alive, or to lie upon dead."

[1]The original of this tale is found in "The Song of the

Lorrainers," a famous poem written by Jehan de Flagy, a minstrel of the twelfth century. In the "Story of Roland" it is supposed to have been related at the court of Charlemagne by a minstrel of Lorraine.

[2]*The vair and the gray*, - furs used for garments, and in heraldry. Vair is the skin of the squirrel, and was arranged in shields of blue and white alternating.

OGIER THE DANE AND THE FAIRIES

When Ogier the Dane was but a babe in his mother's arms, there was heard one day, in his father's castle, the sweetest music that mortals ever listened to. Nobody knew whence the bewitching sounds came; for they seemed to be now here, now there: yet every one was charmed with the delightful melody, and declared that only angels could make music so heavenly. Then suddenly there came into the chamber where Ogier lay six fairies, whose beauty was so wonderful and awful, that none but a babe might gaze upon them without fear. And each of the lovely creatures bore in her hands a garland of the rarest flowers, and rich gifts of gold and gems. And the first fairy took the child in her arms, and kissed him, and said, -

"Better than kingly crown, or lands, or rich heritage, fair babe, I give thee a brave, strong heart. Be fearless as the eagle, and bold as the lion; be the bravest knight among men."

Then the second fairy took the child, and dandled him fondly on her knees, and looked long and lovingly into his clear gray eyes.

"What is genius without opportunity?" said she. "What is a brave heart without the ability to do brave deeds? I give to thee many an opportunity for manly action."

The third fairy laid the dimpled hands of the babe in her own white palm, and stroked softly his golden hair.

"Strong-hearted boy, for whom so many noble deeds are waiting, I, too, will give thee a boon. My gift is skill and strength such as shall never fail thee in fight, nor allow thee to be beaten by a foe. Success to thee, fair Ogier!"

The fourth fairy touched tenderly the mouth and the eyes and the noble brow of the babe.

"Be fair of speech," said she, "be noble in action, be courteous, be kind: these are the gifts I bring thee. For what will a strong heart, or a bold undertaking, or success in every enterprise, avail, unless one has the respect and the love of one's fellow-men?"

Then the fifth fairy came forward, and clasped Ogier in her arms, and held him a long time quietly, without speaking a word. At last she said, -

"The gifts which my sisters have given thee will scarcely bring thee happiness; for, while they add to thy honor, they may make thee dangerous to others. They may lead thee into the practice of selfishness and base acts of tyranny. That man is little to be envied who loves not his fellow-men. The boon, therefore, that I bring thee is the power and the will to esteem others as frail mortals equally deserving with thyself."

And then the sixth fairy, the youngest and the most beautiful of all, who was none other than Morgan le Fay, the Queen of Avalon, caught up the child, and danced about the room in rapturous joy. And, in tones more musical than mortals often hear, she sang a sweet lullaby, a song of fairyland and of the island vale of Avalon, where the souls of heroes dwell.

James Baldwin

And, when she had finished singing, Morgan le Fay crowned the babe with a wreath of laurel and gold, and lighted a fairy torch that she held in her hand. "This torch," said she, "is the measure of thy earthly days; and it shall not cease to burn until thou hast visited me in Avalon, and sat at table with King Arthur and the heroes who dwell there in that eternal summer-land."

Then the fairies gave the babe gently back into his mother's arms, and they strewed the floor of the chamber with many a rich gem and lovely flower; the odor of roses and the sweetest perfumes filled the air, and the music of angels' voices was heard above; and the fairies vanished in a burst of sunbeams, and were seen no more. And when the queen's maidens came soon afterward into the chamber, they found the child smiling in his mother's arms. But she was cold and lifeless: her spirit had flown away to fairyland.

HOW CHARLEMAGNE CROSSED THE ALPS

It was near the time of the solemn festival of Easter, - the time when Nature seems to rise from the grave, and the Earth puts on anew her garb of youth and beauty. King Charlemagne was at St. Omer; for there the good Archbishop Turpin was making ready to celebrate the great feast with more than ordinary grandeur. Thither, too, had come the members of the king's household, and a great number of lords and ladies, the noblest in France.

Scarcely had the good archbishop pronounced a blessing upon the devout multitude assembled at the Easter service, when two messengers came in hot haste, and demanded to speak with the king. They had come from Rome, and they bore letters from Pope Leo. Sad was the news which these letters brought, but it was news which would fire the heart of every Christian knight. The Saracens had landed in Italy, and had taken Rome by assault. "The pope and the cardinals and the legates have fled," said the letters; "the churches are torn down; the holy relics are lost; and the Christians are put to the sword. Wherefore the Holy Father charges you as a Christian king to march at once to the help of the Church."

It needed no word of Charlemagne to arouse the ardor of his warriors. Every other undertaking must be laid aside, so long as Rome and the Church were in danger. And the heralds proclaimed that on the morrow, at break of day,

James Baldwin

the army would move southward toward Italy.

The morning after Easter dawned, and the great army waited for the signal to march. The bugles sounded, and the long line of steel-clad knights and warriors began to move. Charlemagne rode in the front ranks, ready, like a true knight, to brave every difficulty, and to be the first in every post of danger. Never did a better king wear spur.

Great was the haste with which the army moved, and very impatient were the warriors; for the whole of France lay between them and fair Italy, and they knew that weeks of weary marching must be endured, ere they could meet their Pagan foe in battle, and drive him out of the Christians' land.

Many days they rode among the rich fields and between the blooming orchards of the Seine valley; many days they toiled over unbroken forest roads, and among marshes and bogs, and across untrodden moorlands. They climbed steep hills, and swam broad rivers, and endured the rain and the wind and the fierce heat of the noonday sun, and sometimes even the pangs of hunger and thirst. But they carried brave hearts within them; and they comforted themselves with the thought that all their suffering was for the glory of God and the honor of the king, for their country's safety and the security of their homes.

Every day, as they advanced, the army increased in numbers and in strength: for the news had been carried all over the land, that the Saracens had taken Rome, and that Charlemagne with his host was hastening to the rescue; and knights and noblemen from every city and town and country-side came to join his standard, sometimes alone and singly, and sometimes with a great retinue of fighting men and servitors. When at last they had passed the boundaries of France, and only the great mountains lay between them and Italy, Charlemagne could look behind him, and see an army of a hundred thousand men. And now messengers came to him again, urging him to hasten with all speed to the succor of the pope.

But the Alps Mountains lifted themselves up in his pathway, and their snowy crags frowned threateningly upon him; their steep, rocky sides arose like walls before him, and seemed to forbid his going farther; and there appeared to be no way of reaching Italy, save by a long and circuitous route through the southern passes.

In the hope that he might find some shorter and easier passage, Charlemagne now sent out scouts and mountaineers to explore every valley and gorge, and every seeming mountain pass. But all came back with the same story: there was not even so much as a path up which the mountain goats could clamber, much less a road broad enough for an army, with horses and baggage, to traverse. The king was in despair, and he called together his counsellors and wise men to consider what should be done. Duke Namon urged that they should march around by way of the southern passes; for, although a full month would thus be lost, yet there was no other safe and well-known land-route to Italy. Ganelon advised that they should turn back, and, marching to Marseilles, embark from thence on ships, and undertake to reach Rome by way of the sea.

Then the dwarf Malagis came before Charlemagne, bearing in his hand a book, from which he read many spells and weird enchantments. Upon the ground he drew with his wand a magic ring, and he laid therein the hammer of Thor and the sword of Mahomet. In a loud, commanding voice, he called upon the sprites, the trolls, and the goblins, with whom he was familiar, to come at

James Baldwin

once into his presence. Forthwith the lightning flashed, and the thunder rolled, and smoke and fire burst forth from the mountain peaks, and the rocks and great ice-fields were loosened among the crags, and came tumbling down into the valley. Dwarfs and elves, and many an uncanny thing, danced and shouted in the mountain caves; grinning ogres peeped out from the deep clefts and gorges; and the very air seemed full of ghost-like creatures. Then the wizard called by name a wise but wicked goblin, known among the Saracens as Ashtaroth; and the goblin came at once, riding in a whirlwind, and feeling very angry because he was obliged to obey.

"Tell me now," said Malagis, "and tell me truly, whether there is here so much as a pathway by which Charlemagne may lead his army through the mountains."

The goblin was silent for a moment; a dark cloud rested upon his face, and his look was terrible. But the wizard, in no wise daunted, returned his glance, and in the tones of a master bade him clear up that clouded look, and answer the question he had asked. Then Ashtaroth curbed his anger, and spoke:

"On what errand would the French king cross the Alps?" he asked. "Seeks he not to harm my friends the Saracens?"

"That is, indeed, his errand," answered Malagis.

"Then, why should I do aught to help him?" asked the goblin. "Why do you call me from my rest, and bid me betray my friends?"

"That is not for thee to ask," said Malagis. "I have called thee as a master calls his slave. Tell me now, and tell me truly, is there here any pass across the mountains into Italy?"

"There is such a pass," answered the goblin gravely; "but it is hidden to eyes like mine. I cannot guide you to it, nor can any of my kind show you how to find it. It is a pathway which only the pure can tread."

"Tell me one thing more," said Malagis. "Tell me one thing, and I will let thee go. How prosper thy friends the Saracens at Rome?"

"They have taken all but the Capitol," was the answer. "They have slain many Christians, and burned many buildings. The pope and the cardinals have fled. If Charlemagne reach not Italy within a month, ill will it fare with his friends."

Then Malagis, satisfied with what he had heard, unwound the spell of his enchantments; and amid a cloud of fire and smoke the goblin flew back into the mountains.

Next the good Turpin came forward, with a crosier in his hand, and a bishop's mitre on his head, and a long white robe thrown over his shoulders, scarcely hiding the steel armor which he wore beneath. He lifted up his eyes to heaven and prayed. And the sound of his voice arose among the cliffs, and resounded among the rocks, and was echoed from valley to valley, and re-echoed among the peaks and crags, and carried over the mountain tops, even to the blue sky above. The king and those who stood about him fancied that they heard sweet strains of music issuing from the mountain caves; the most bewitching sounds arose among the rocks and gorges; the air was filled with a heavenly perfume and the songs of birds; and a holy calm settled over mountain and valley, and fell like a blessing upon the earth. Then the Alps no longer seemed obstacles in their way. The steep cliffs, which had been like mighty walls barring their progress, seemed now mere gentle slopes, rising little by little toward heaven, and affording a pleasant and easy highway to the fair fields of Italy beyond.

While Charlemagne and his peers gazed in rapt delight upon this vision, there came down from the mountain crags a beautiful creature such as none of them had ever before seen. It was a noble stag, white as the drifted snow, his head crowned with wide-branching antlers, from every point of which bright sunbeams seemed to flash.

"Behold our leader and our hope!" cried Turpin. "Behold the sure-footed guide which the Wonder-king has sent to lead us through narrow ways, and over dangerous steeps, to the smiling valleys and fields of Italy! Be only strong and trustful and believing, and a safe way shall open for us, even where there seemed to be no way."

Then the vision faded slowly away from the sight of the peers; and the mountain walls rose up before them as grim and steep as ever; and the snow-crowned crags looked down upon them even more angrily than before, and there seemed no road nor pathway which the foot of man could follow. But the wondrous white stag, which had filled their minds with a new-born hope, still stood in plain sight on the lowermost slopes of the mountain.

The king, without once taking his eyes from the Heaven-sent creature, mounted his war-steed, and sounded the bugle which hung at his girdle; and the great army, confiding in the wisdom of their leader, began to move. The white stag went first, steadily following a narrow pathway, which led upward by many steep ascents, seemingly to the very clouds; and behind him rode Charlemagne, keeping ever in view his radiant, hopeful guide, and followed by the long line of knights and warriors, who, cheered by his earnest faith, never once feared the end.

Higher and higher they climbed, and more and more difficult became the way. On one side of them arose a steep wall, shutting out from their sight more than half of the sky; on the other side, dark gorges and yawning gulfs descended, threatening to bury the whole army in their bottomless depths. And by and by they came to the region of snow and ice, where the Storm-king holds his court, and reigns in ever-lasting solitude. Looking back, they could see sweet France, lying spread out as a map beneath them, its pleasant fields and its busy towns seeming only as specks in the dim distance. But when they looked forward, hoping there to see a like map of fair Italy, only the rocks and the ice, and the narrow pathway, and the desolate mountain crags, met their sight.

They would have become disheartened by the difficulties before them, and have turned back in utter despair, had not the bright form of their guide, and the cheerful countenance of Charlemagne, inspired them with ever-renewed hope. For seven days they toiled among the dangerous steeps; and on the eighth a glorious vision burst upon their view - the smiling plains of Italy lay before them.

At this sight a great shout of joy went up from the throats of the toil-worn heroes, and the good archbishop returned thanks to Heaven for their deliverance from peril. And, a few hours later, the whole army emerged into the pleasant valleys of Piedmont, and encamped not far from Aosta.

James Baldwin

WHAT HAPPENED AT RONCEVAUX

In all the world there was not such another king as Charlemagne. Wherever his arms were carried, there victory followed; and neither Pagan nor haughty Christian foe dared lift up hands any more against him. His kingdom stretched from the Baltic Sea to the Italian shores, and from beyond the Rhine to the great Western Ocean. Princes were his servants; kings were his vassals; and even the Pope of Rome did him homage. And now he had crossed the Pyrenees, and was carrying fire and sword into the fair fields and rich towns of the Spanish Moors; for he had vowed to punish Marsilius, king of Spain, for the injuries he had done the French in former years. He had overrun the whole of that haughty land, and had left neither castle, nor city, nor wall, unbroken, save only the town of Saragossa.

One day Charlemagne sat beneath the blossoming trees of an orchard near Cordova. White was his beard, and flowered was his head; yet still handsome was his body, and proud his form. Around him were the noblest of knights, Roland and Oliver and old Duke Namon, and fifteen thousand of the choicest men of France. It was a gala-day for the French, and the warriors amused themselves with field sports, and many pleasant games. Then a party of Moorish messengers were brought before the king. They came from Marsilius at Saragossa, who had sent to beg peace of Charlemagne.

"What will Marsilius give for peace?" asked the king.

"If you will go back to your own country, and cease this unhappy war," answered they, "then Marsilius binds himself to do this: he will go to Aix at Michaelmas, and be baptized; he will do homage then for Spain, and will faithfully hold it in fief from you; he will give you great store of treasures, - four hundred mules loaded with gold, and fifty cart-loads of silver, besides numbers of bears and lions and tame greyhounds, and seven hundred camels, and a thousand moulted falcons. Too long has this cruel war been waging. Marsilius would fain have peace."

Charlemagne listened to the words of the messengers, but he was not quick to answer. He called together his peers, and laid the matter before them.

"What think you of the Moor's offers of peace?" asked he.

"Put no trust in Marsilius!" cried Roland. "He is the most faithless of Pagans, and speaks only lies. Carry on the war as you have begun, and talk not of peace until Saragossa is ours."

Charlemagne's face grew dark, yet he said not a word. It was plain that he coveted the treasures which Marsilius had promised. Then Ganelon arose, and with curling lip, thus answered, -

"If Marsilius offers to do fealty for Spain, and to hold it as a gift from you, wherefore should we refuse his plea? He who would advise you otherwise cares not what manner of death we die."

And Namon of Bavaria added, "If the Moor is beaten, and cries for mercy, it would be an unknightly act to continue warring against him. My voice is for peace."

James Baldwin

And all the peers, save Roland and Oliver, cried out, "The duke hath spoken wisely. Let us have peace!"

"It is well," answered Charlemagne, "and so it shall be. But whom shall we send to Saragossa to treat with Marsilius, and to receive the pledges of good faith which he shall give?"

Then arose a great dispute among the peers as to which should undertake this dangerous errand. Duke Namon, who was never known to shirk a duty, offered to go; but the king would not consent. He liked not to part with his wise old friend, even for a single day.

"I will carry the message," said Roland.

"Not so, my brother," interrupted Oliver. "Thy pride will get the better of thy judgment, and thou wilt act rashly. Let me undertake the errand."

But Charlemagne refused them both. "Neither of you shall go," said he. "But you may choose one from among these other barons to be the messenger."

"Then send Ganelon of Mayence," said Roland. "He is in favor of this peace, and he is most fit to carry the message."

"Yes, send Ganelon of Mayence!" cried all the peers.

Ganelon rose from his seat in rage. Fire flashed from his hazel eyes; his lips quivered; he tore the sable border from his crimson tunic, and stood proudly before Roland. "Fool!" cried he. "Who art thou who wouldst send me to Marsilius? If I but live to come again from Saragossa, I will deal thee such a blow as thou shalt never forget."

"Speak softly, Sir Ganelon," said Roland. "Men know that I care not for threats. If thou art afraid of the danger, mayhap the king will allow me to go in thy place."

Hotter than before was Ganelon's wrath; but he held his tongue, and turned humbly toward the king.

"My lord," said he, "since you will that I bear this message toMarsilius, I go. But I know too well the false-hearted Moor to hope that I shall ever return. I pray you, care for my fair son Baldwin, to whom I leave my lands and all my fiefs. Keep him well, for these eyes of mine shall never see him again."

"Thou art too fearful, and too tender of heart," said the king, as he offered to Ganelon the staff and the glove which messengers were wont to carry as signs of their office. "Go now, and doubt not the issue of thine errand."

Ganelon took the staff; but his hand trembled, and the glove fell to the ground.

"An evil omen is that," whispered the peers who saw it. "It is a sign of no good fortune, either to him or to us."

Then Ganelon bade the king good-by, and went on his way. But he said to himself, "This is Roland's doings, and I shall hate him all my life long: neither shall I love Oliver his brother, nor any other of the twelve peers."

When he reached Saragossa, Ganelon was led into the presence of Marsilius. The Moorish king sat under a pine tree, and twenty thousand warriors stood around him.

"What answer bring you from your liege-lord Charle-magne?" asked he.

James Baldwin

Ganelon had studied well what he should say; and he answered, like one long used to cunning guile, "If thou wilt be baptized and become a Christian, Charlemagne will give thee the half of Spain to hold in fief. If thou wilt not accept this offer, then he will besiege thee in Saragossa, and take thee prisoner; and he will send thee bound upon the back of a sumter horse to Aix, and there he will have thee put to death. This is the message which Charlemagne sends thee."

Great was the anger of the Moorish king, and he raised his javelin to strike the messenger dead. But Ganelon, no whit daunted, set his back against the trunk of a tree, and drew his sword part way from its scabbard.

"Good sword," said he, "thou art fair and bright, and thou hast done me many a service. Never shall it be said that Ganelon died alone in a strange land."

But the courtiers of King Marsilius stepped in between them. "It were better," said they, "to treat with this man than to slay him. If his face slander him not, he is a man who may be persuaded to help us. Try him."

Then Marsilius called Ganelon to his side, and offered him five hundred pounds of gold for his friendship. And the two sat long together, and plotted bloodshed and treason.

"Indeed, what think you of this Charlemagne?" asked the Moor. "Through how many lands has he carried that old body of his? How many scars are there on his shield? How many kingdoms has he stolen, and how many kings impoverished? Methinks that his days are well-nigh spent. He must be more than two hundred years old."

But Ganelon, although a traitor, would say naught against

the king.

"None can see him," said he, "but will say that he is a man. None can so praise or honor him, but that there shall yet be in him more worth and goodness."

"Yet, methinks," said the Moor, "that he is very old. His beard is white; his hair is flowered. It is strange that he grows not tired of fighting."

"That he will never do so long as Roland, his nephew, lives," answered Ganelon. "There, too, is Oliver; and there are the other peers of the realm, all of whom the king holds most dear. They alone are worth twenty thousand men."

"I have heard much of Roland," said the Moor; "and I would fain put him out of the way. Tell me how it can be done, and thou shalt have three baggage-horse loads of gold, three of silver, and three of fine silk and red wine and jewels."

Now Ganelon desired, above all things, the death of Roland; and he eagerly made known his plans to Marsilius.

"Send to Charlemagne," said he, "great store of rich gifts, so that every Frenchman shall wonder at your wealth. Send also hostages, and promise him that on next Michaelmas you will be baptized at Aix and do him homage for Spain. Pleased with your promises, he will return to France. But his rear-guard, with Roland and Oliver, and twenty thousand Frenchmen, will be long among the passes of the Pyrenees. A hundred thousand Moors could well cope with them there."

Then the two traitors exchanged promises and pledges;

and Ganelon, taking with him the keys of Saragossa, and rich presents for Charlemagne, went back to Cordova.

Right glad was Charlemagne to hear the message which the lying traitor brought. He was tired of warring, and he longed to return in peace to his own sweet France. The next day the trumpets sounded throughout the camp. The tents were struck; the baggage was packed on the sumter horses; the knights mounted their steeds; banners and pennons waved thick in the air; the great army began its glad march home-ward. Joyful was the beginning of that march; but, ah, how sad the ending! The French did not see the crafty Moors following them through the upper valleys, their banners furled, their helmets closed, their lances in rest.

That first night the king was troubled with sad dreams. He thought that Ganelon seized his lance and shook it, and that it fell in pieces. He thought that he hunted in the forest of Ardennes, and that both a boar and a leopard attacked him. A thousand fearful fancies vexed him. Mountains fell upon him and crushed him; the earth yawned and swallowed him; perils beset him on every side: but amid them all, the face of Ganelon was ever to be seen.

By and by the army came to the Pyrenees, and the great land of France lay just beyond the mountains.

"To whom now," said the king to his peers, "shall we intrust our rear-guard while we pass safely through the mountain gates?"

"Give It to Roland, your nephew," said Ganelon. "There is none more worthy than he."

"And who shall lead the vanguard?"

"Ogier, the Dane. Next to Roland, he is the bravest of your barons."

Right willingly did Roland accept the dangerous trust.

"I will see to it," said he, "that no harm come to the French while passing through the gates. Neither pack-horse, nor mule, nor palfrey, nor charger, nor man shall we lose, that shall not be paid for by the blood of our foes."

Then he mounted his steed, and rode back to the rear. And with him went Oliver and Turpin the archbishop, and twenty thousand valiant fighting-men.

High were the mountains, and gloomy the valleys; dark were the rocks, and fearful were the glens. But the day was fair, and the sky was clear; and the bright shields of the warriors glittered in the sunlight like flashes of fire. All at once a sound, as of a thousand trumpets blowing, was heard in the valley below them. The French knights hearkened.

"Comrades," said Oliver, "methinks that we are followed by the Moors."

"And may God grant us battle and victory!" said Roland earnestly. "Well is it that we are here to defend the king. For one should never murmur that he suffers distress for his friends: for them, he should lose, if need be, both blood and flesh and even life itself."

Then Oliver climbed a high pine tree, and looked down into the grassy valley behind them. There he beheld such troops of Pagan folk as he had never seen before.

"Comrades," cried he, "we shall have such a battle as no

man has known. The passes are full of armed Moors: their hauberks and glittering helmets fill the lower valleys. Great mischief is in store for us, but may we stand to the field like men!"

"Shame be to him that flees!" said the warriors who heard him.

Bewildered and amazed at sight of so terrible an array of Pagans, Oliver descended from the tree.

"Brother Roland," said he, "I pray thee blow thy horn. The king will hear it, and he will turn him about and come to our succor."

"To do so would be to act as a craven," answered Roland. "Never shall it be said that I feared a foe. I will strike strong strokes with my sword, Durandal. Ill shall it fare with the Pagan traitors."

"Comrade Roland," again said Oliver, "now blow thy horn. Charlemagne will hear it, and he will make his host return."

"Never," answered Roland, "shall my kinsmen upbraid me, or be blamed for me. But I will strike with Durandal. The brand which the king gave me when he knighted me, that shall be our succor."

Then Oliver prayed him the third time, "Comrade Roland, sound now thine ivory horn. Charlemagne, who is passing the gates, will hear us and come to our aid."

"No man shall ever say," answered Roland, "that I have blown my horn for Pagans. My kinsmen shall not bear that reproach. But when the great battle is joined, then you shall see the lightning flashes of Durandal in the thickest of the fight. A thousand and seven hundred times shall the blade be dyed in the blood of the Moors. Better would it be to perish than suffer shame."

But Oliver was not yet satisfied. "I have seen the Moorish host," said he. "The mountains and the plains, the valleys and the groves, are full of them. Never have we fought against such great odds."

"Friend and brother," answered Roland, "say not another word. The king has left us here, with a rear-guard of twenty thousand men, and he esteems every one of us a hero. Do thou strike with thy lance and thy good blade Haultclear. As for me, Durandal shall serve me well. And, if I die, men shall say, 'This sword belonged to a noble knight.'"

Then the good Archbishop Turpin rode down the ranks, holding a sword in one hand and a crucifix in the other. "Comrades," cried he, "the king has left us here. He trusts in us, and for him we shall die. Cry now your sins to Heaven. Pray God's mercy, and ask His blessing."

In a moment every knight among those twenty thousand horsemen had dismounted. Humbly and reverently every knee was bent, and every head was bowed. And the good archbishop blessed the company in God's name.

"If ye die," said he, "ye shall have places in paradise."

Then the warriors arose, light-hearted and hopeful. They rode into the place which is called Roncevaux, the Vale of Thorns, and there they put themselves in battle array, and waited the onset of their foes. Roland sat astride of his good war steed, and proudly faced the Moorish host. In his hand he held the bared blade Durandal, pointing toward heaven. Never was seen a more comely knight.

James Baldwin

Courteously he spoke to the warriors about him. Then, putting spurs to his steed, he cried,

"Comrades, ride onward! The day shall be ours!"

"Forget not the war cry of Charlemagne," said Oliver.

At these words the rocks and valleys rang with the cry, "Monjoie! Monjoie!" And every warrior dashed forward to meet the foe.

Long and fierce was the fight, and terrible was the slaughter. With heart and strength the French knights struck. The Moors were slain by hundreds and by thousands. For a time victory seemed to be with the French. Many and valiant were the deeds achieved by Roland and Oliver and the archbishop and the peers that were with them. But at length Marsilius came down upon them with a fresh troop of seven thousand Moors. They hemmed the French heroes in on every side. Roland saw his knights falling one by one around him. All were slain save sixty men.

"Oliver, my fair dear comrade," said he, "behold how many brave vassals have fallen! The battle goes hard with us. If, now, we only knew how to send news to Charlemagne, he would return and succor us."

"It is too late," answered Oliver. "Better would we die than suffer shame."

Then said Roland, "I will sound my ivory horn. Mayhap Charlemagne, who is passing the gates of Spain, will hear it and return."

"Do no such thing," answered Oliver. "Great shame would be upon you and your kinsmen forever. You would not blow your horn when I advised it, and now you shall not do so because the day is lost."

Then the archbishop rode up, and said, "The day is indeed lost, and to blow the horn would now no more avail us. But, should the king hear it, he will come back through the passes. He will find us dead: his men will lift us in biers and carry us home to be buried in minsters, and we shall not be left as food for wolves and dogs."

"Thou sayest well," said Roland. And he placed the horn to his lips. High were the hills, deep and dark were the gorges, narrow were the ways among the mountains. Yet the sound of that horn was heard for thirty leagues. Charlemagne and Duke Namon heard it while yet they were between the gates.

"Hark!" said the king. "I hear Roland's horn. The felon Moors have attacked him: he is hard pressed in battle."

"You are foolishly mistaken," said Ganelon. "There is no battle. You are old, your beard is white, your head is flowery, you are growing childish. You love your silly nephew, Roland, too well. He is only hunting among the mountains. He would blow his horn all day for a single hare, and then he would boast before you of his valor. Ride on. Your own France is not far ahead."

But the king was not to be deceived. He ordered Ganelon to be seized and bound and given in charge of his cooks, who were to hold him a close prisoner. They bound him with a great chain, and laid him across the back of a sumter horse; they pulled his beard; they struck him with their fists; they beat him with sticks. Sorry indeed was the traitor's plight, but his punishment was just. As for Charlemagne, he turned and with all his host hastened back to the succor of Roland and the valiant rear-guard.

High were the mountain walls, and darkly did they overhang the way; deep were the mountain gorges; swift and strong were the torrents; narrow and steep was the road. The trumpets sounded: anxiously and with haste the king and his horsemen retraced their steps.

Fiercely still the battle raged in the fated Vale of Thorns. One by one the French knights fell; but for every one that was slain ten Pagans bit the dust. At length Oliver was wounded unto death; but still he sat on his horse and struck valiantly about him with his good Haultclear. His eyes lost their strength: he could not see. He met Roland, and struck him a blow which split his helmet down to the nose-piece, but luckily wounded him not.

"Brother," said Roland softly and gently, "thou hast not done this willingly. I am Roland, he who has loved thee so long and so well."

"Ah, comrade!" said Oliver, "I hear thee; but I cannot see thee. Pray forgive me if I have harmed thee."

"I am none the worse," answered Roland; "and there is naught to forgive."

Then the two brothers bent over from their steeds, and embraced each other; and amid much love and many hasty words of farewell, they parted.

And now all the French were slain, save only Roland and the archbishop. The hero was wounded in a dozen places: he felt his life-blood oozing away. Again he drew his ivory horn, and feebly sounded it. He would fain know whether Charlemagne were coming. The king was in the pass, not far away, and he heard the failing blast.

"Ah, Roland!" said he, "the battle goes ill with thee."

Then he turned to his host, and said, "Blow loud your trumpets, that the hero may know that succor comes."

At once sixty thousand bugles were blown so loudly that the valley and the caves resounded, and the rocks themselves trembled. Roland heard it and thanked God. The Pagans heard it and knew that it boded no good to them. They rushed in a body upon Roland and the archbishop. Roland's horse was slain beneath him; his shield was split in twain; his hauberk was broken. The archbishop was mortally wounded, and stretched upon the ground. Again the trumpets of Charlemagne's host were heard, and the Pagans fled in great haste toward Spain.

Then Roland knelt by the side of the dying archbishop. "Kind friend, so good and true," said he, "now the end has come. Our comrades whom we held so dear are all dead. Give me leave to bring them and lay them in order by thee, that we may all have thy blessing."

"It is well," answered the good Turpin. "Do as thou wilt. The field is thine and mine."

So Roland, weak and faint, went all alone through that field of blood, seeking his friends. He found Berenger and Otho and Anseis and Samson, and proud Gerard of Roussillon; and one by one he brought them and laid them on the grass before the archbishop. And lastly he brought back Oliver, pressed gently against his bosom, and placed him on a shield by the others. The archbishop wept; and he lifted up his feeble hands and blessed them: "Sad has it been with you, comrades. May God, the glorious King, receive your souls in His paradise!"

Then Roland, faint with loss of blood, and overcome with grief, swooned and fell to the ground. The good archbishop felt such distress as he had never known before. He staggered to his feet; he took the ivory horn in his hands, and went to fetch water from the brook which flows through the Vale of Thorns. Slowly and feebly he tottered onward, but not far: his strength failed and he fell to the ground. Soon Roland recovered from his swoon and looked about him. On the green grass this side of the rivulet, he saw the archbishop lying. The good Turpin was dead.

And now Roland felt that he, too, was nigh death's door. He took the ivory horn in one hand, and Durandal in the other, and went up a little hill that lies toward Spain. He sat down beneath a pine tree where were four great blocks of marble. He looked at the blade Durandal. "Ha, Durandal," he said, "how bright and white thou art! Thou shinest and flamest against the sun! Many countries have I conquered with thee, and now for thee I have great grief. Better would it be to destroy thee than to have thee fall into the hands of the Pagan folk."

With great effort he raised himself on his feet again. Ten times he smote with Durandal the great rock before him. But the sword was bright and whole as ever, while the rock was split in pieces. Then the hero lay down upon the grass, with his face toward the foe. He put the sword and the horn under him. He stretched his right glove toward heaven, and an unseen hand came and took it away. Dead was the matchless hero.

Not long after this King Charlemagne with his host came to the death-strewn Vale of Thorns. Great was the grief of the king and of all the French, when they found that they had come too late to save even a single life. Roland was found lying on the grass, his face turned toward Spain. Charlemagne took him up tenderly in his arms, and wept.

"Friend Roland," said he, "worthiest of men, bravest of

warriors, noblest of all my knights, what shall I, say when they in France shall ask news of thee? I shall tell them that thou art dead in Spain. With great sorrow shall I hold my realm from this time on. Every day I shall weep and bewail thee, and wish that my life, too, were ended."

Then the French buried their dead on the field where they had fallen. But the king brought Roland and Oliver and the archbishop to Blaye in France, and laid them in white marble tombs; and there they lie until this day in the beautiful little chapel of St. Roman's. And he took the ivory horn to Bordeaux, and filled it with fine gold, and laid it on the altar of the church in that city; and there it is still seen by the pious pilgrims who visit that place.

James Baldwin

VOCABULARY OF PROPER NAMES

Ac ar nā' nǐ a, the most western province of ancient Greece.

A chǐl' lēs (á kǐl' lēz), the ideal hero of the Greeks.

Ae' gir (a' jǐr), in Norse legends, the ruler of the sea.

Ag a mē' dēs (-dēz), one of the architects of the temple at Delphi.

Ag a měm' non, king of Mycenae and leader of the Greeks.

Aix (āks), a city of France, favorite residence of Charlemagne.

A' jǎx, a Greek hero second only to Achilles.

Al ex ǎn' drǒs, a name applied to Paris, prince of Troy.

Al phē' ǔs, a hunter transformed into a river of Greece.

Al thē' a, queen of Calydon, mother of Meleager.

A mǐl' ǐ as, a mythical smith of Burgundy.

And' vä rï, a dwarf, the keeper of the Rhine treasure.

An tǐl' o chus (-kus), a Greek prince and friend of Achilles.

A ǒs' tä, a town in northern Italy.

Aph ro dī' tē, in Greek mythology, the goddess of love.

A pŏl' lo, in Greek mythology, the god of music, poetry, and healing.

Ar cā' dĭ a, a mountainous country in Greece.

Ardennes (är dĕn'), a forest in northern France.

Ar e thū' sa, a nymph loved by Alpheus.

Ar' go, the ship that carried Jason and his companions.

Ar' tē nĭs, twin sister of Apollo; goddess of the woods.

Ar' thur, a heroic legendary king of Britain.

As' as (äs åz), the gods of the North.

As' gärd, in Norse mythology, the home of the gods or Asas.

Ash' ta rŏth, an evil spirit.

At a lăn' ta, an Arcadian princess and swift-footed huntress.

A the' na, the goddess of knowledge, arts, and sciences.

At' ro pŏs, one of the three Fates.

Au' lis, a town on the east coast of Greece.

Au tŏl' y cus, a famous Greek chieftain, grandfather of Odysseus.

Av' a lon, fairyland (in mediaeval legends).

Băl' ĭ os, "Swift," one of the horses given to Peleus.

Bäl' mŭng, the sword of Siegfried.

Bē' a trĭce, the wife of Eego of Belin.

Be gō' (bā gō'), duke of Belin and feudal chief of Gascony.

Ber en ger' (-än zhā'), a friend of Bego.

Blaye (blā), a seaport of France, 21 miles from Bordeaux.

Bō' re as, the North Wind.

Bor deaux' (-dō'), a city on west coast of France.

Bŭr' gun dy, a duchy including a part of northeastern France.

Căl' chas (kăl' kăl), a soothsayer of Mycense.

Căl' y don, a city in ancient Greece.

Cas san' dra, a prophetess, the daughter of Priam.

Cas tor, twin brother of Pollux and brother of Helen.

Cĕn' taur, one of an ancient race inhabiting the country near Mount Pelion, said to have the bodies of horses.

Charlemagne (shär' le mān), king of the Franks, 742-814.

Cheiron (kī' ron), a Centaur famed for his wisdom.

Clē ō pā' tra, the wife of Meleager.

Clō' thō, one of the three Fates.

Clyt' em nĕs tra, the wife of Agamemnon.

Crete (krēt), an island southeast of Greece.

Crĭs' sa, a gulf in Greece, now called Gulf of Corinth.

Där' da nus, ancestor of the people of Troy.

Dē' lŏs, a small island east of Greece.

Dĕl' phī, a town at the foot of Mount Parnassus, the seat of the oracle of Apollo.

Dū răn' dal, the sword of Roland.

E' lis, a country in southern Greece.

E' rin, the ancient name for Ireland.

E' ris, the goddess of discord.

Euboea (u bē' a), a large island east of Greece.

Fäf' nïr, a dragon that guarded the Rhine treasure.

Fa năn' der, a cataract referred to in Norse mythology.

Frō mōnt', duke of Bordeaux.

Gä' ne lon, a duke of Mayence noted for his treachery.

Gä rin' (-rănh), one of the sons of Bego of Belia.

Găs' cō ny, an ancient duchy of France.

Gerin (zhẽ rănh'), a brother of Bego of Belio.

Hā' dēs, the land of the shades, or of the dead.

Hault' clear, the sword of Oliver.

He' bē, the goddess of youth and spring.

Hĕc' tor, a prince of Troy, son of Priam.

Hĕl' en, the wife of Menelaus, celebrated for her beauty.

He lō ïse' (hā lō ēz'), the sister of Bego of Belin.

He' ra, the wife of Zeus; often called Juno.

Her' cu lēs (-lēz), a mighty hero of the Golden Age of Greece.

Her' mēs (-mēz), the messenger of the gods; same as Mercury.

Her nau din (her nō dănh'), a son of Bego.

He sī' o nē, a princess of Troy, sister of Priam.

Haenir (he' nïr), a companion of Odio.

Hreidmar (hrīd' mar), the father of Regin.

Hū' na land, a country mentioned in Norse mythology.

Hy per bō' re ans, the people who lived beyond the North Wind.

I ä' sus, a king of Arcadia, father of Atalanta.

I' das, the father of Cleopatra.

I dŏm' e neūs, a king of Crete, friend of Menelaus.

Il' ĭ os, the same as Troy; Ilium.

I' lus, the founder of Ilios or Troy.

Iph ĭ ge nī' a, a princess, the daughter of Agamemnon.

I' ris, a messenger of the gods, personification of the rainbow.

Jā' son, a Greek hero, the leader of the Argonauts.

Kwä' ser, in Norse mythology, a being noted for his wisdom.

Lăc e dae' mon (lăs-), an ancient Greek city, same as Sparta.

Lăch' e sĭs (lăk-), one of the three Fates.

La ŏm' e don, a king of Troy, father of Priam.

Lō' kī, in Norse mythology, the spirit of mischief.

Lōr rāine', a region on the border between France and Germany.

Ma hŏm' et, an Arab, the founder of Mohammedanism.

Măi' a gis (-zhē), a dwarf enchanter and magician.

Mär seilles' (-sālz), a city of France on the Mediterranean.

Mär sïl' ĭ us, a Moorish king of Spain.

Mayence (mä yŏns'), a city on the Rhine River.

Mĕl e ā' ger (-jēr), a Greek hero, prince of Calydon.

Mï' mer, in Norse mythology, the possessor of the well of wisdom.

Môr' gan le Fāy, the queen of the fairies.

My cē' nae, a city of ancient Greece.

Nä' mōn, Charlemagne's most trusted counsellor.

Nē' rēus, "the old man of the sea," father of the sea nymphs.

Nĕs' tor, king of Pylos, oldest of the Greek heroes at Troy.

O' dĭn, in Norse mythology the chief of the gods.

O dys' seūs, the wisest of the Greek heroes; same as Ulysses.

Oenone (ē nō' ne), a river nymph, the wife of Paris.

Ogier (ō zhā), a Danish hero under Charlemagne.

Oi' neūs, a king of Calydon, father of Meleager.

Ol' ĭ ver, one of Charlemagne's paladins, comrade of Roland,

O lym' pus, a mountain in Greece, the home of the gods.

O rĕs' tēs, the son of Agamemnon.

Orleans (ŏr lā ŏn'), an important city in France.

Or sĭl' o chus, a king of the ancient city of Pherae.

Pal a mē' dēs, a Greek hero in the war with Troy.

Păr' is, a prince of Troy, second son of Priam.

Pär nas' sus, a mountain in Greece near Delphi.

Pē' leūs, the father of Achilles.

Pē' lĭ on, a mountain on the east coast of Greece.

Pĕp' in, a king of the Franks, father of Charlemagne.

Phoe' bus, another name for Apollo.

Piēd' mŏnt, a district in northern Italy.

Pŏl' lux, the twin brother of Castor, and brother of Helen.

Po seī' don, supreme lord of the sea; same as Neptune.

Prī' am, the last king of Troy.

Pū ĕlle', an ancient forest in France.

Py' los, an ancient town in the south part of Greece.

Pyr' e nees, the mountains between France and Spain.

Py' thon, the serpent slain by Apollo.

Rän, in Norse mythology, the goddess of the sea.

Re' gin (-jĭn), a dwarf, the instructor of Siegfried.

Rō' land, the most famous of Charlemagne's paladins.

Ronce vaux' (-vō), a valley in Navarre, Spain, in the Pyrenees.

Roussillon (roo sē' yôn'), an ancient district of France.

St. Omer (sĕn tō mâr'), a famous city in northern France.

St. Quentin (sâăn kŏn tăn'), a city in northeastern France.

Săl a mis, an island of ancient Greece.

Sar' a cens, the Arab followers of Mohammed.

Scae' an (skē' an), the principal gate of Troy.

Sca măn' der, a river near Troy.

Seine (sān), one of the principal rivers of France.

Sieg' frīēd, a mythical hero of the Rhine country.

Sï' gyn, the wife of Loki.

Skä de, in Norse mythology, the goddess of the snow.

Tĕl' a mon, a Greek hero, the father of Ajax.

Thes sā' lĭ an, belonging to Thessaly in northern Greece.

Thē' tis, a sea nymph, the mother of Achilles.

Tro phō' nĭ us, one of the architects of the temple at Delphi.

Tûr' pin, archbishop of Rheims, and paladin of Charlemagne.

Valenciennes (vä lŏn syĕn'), a city in northeastern France.

Vŭl' can, the blacksmith of the gods.

Xanthos (zăn' thus), "Old Gold," one of the horses of Peleus.

Zeūs, the king of the gods; same as Jupiter.

Choose from Thousands of 1stWorldLibrary Classics By

A. M. Barnard	C. M. Ingleby	Elizabeth Gaskell
Ada Leverson	Carolyn Wells	Elizabeth McCracken
Adolphus William Ward	Catherine Parr Traill	Elizabeth Von Arnim
Aesop	Charles A. Eastman	Ellem Key
Agatha Christie	Charles Amory Beach	Emerson Hough
Alexander Aaronsohn	Charles Dickens	Emilie F. Carlen
Alexander Kielland	Charles Dudley Warner	Emily Dickinson
Alexandre Dumas	Charles Farrar Browne	Enid Bagnold
Alfred Gatty	Charles Ives	Enilor Macartney Lane
Alfred Ollivant	Charles Kingsley	Erasmus W. Jones
Alice Duer Miller	Charles Klein	Ernie Howard Pie
Alice Turner Curtis	Charles Hanson Towne	Ethel May Dell
Alice Dunbar	Charles Lathrop Pack	Ethel Turner
Allen Chapman	Charles Romyn Dake	Ethel Watts Mumford
Ambrose Bierce	Charles Whibley	Eugenie Foa
Amelia E. Barr	Charles Willing Beale	Eugene Wood
Amory H. Bradford	Charlotte M. Braeme	Eustace Hale Ball
Andrew Lang	Charlotte M. Yonge	Evelyn Everett-green
Andrew McFarland Davis	Charlotte Perkins Stetson	Everard Cotes
Andy Adams	Clair W. Hayes	F. H. Cheley
Anna Alice Chapin	Clarence Day Jr.	F. J. Cross
Anna Sewell	Clarence E. Mulford	F. Marion Crawford
Annie Besant	Clemence Housman	Federick Austin Ogg
Annie Hamilton Donnell	Confucius	Ferdinand Ossendowski
Annie Payson Call	Coningsby Dawson	Francis Bacon
Annie Roe Carr	Cornelis DeWitt Wilcox	Francis Darwin
Annonaymous	Cyril Burleigh	Frances Hodgson Burnett
Anton Chekhov	D. H. Lawrence	Frances Parkinson Keyes
Arnold Bennett	Daniel Defoe	Frank Gee Patchin
Arthur Conan Doyle	David Garnett	Frank Harris
Arthur M. Winfield	Dinah Craik	Frank Jewett Mather
Arthur Ransome	Don Carlos Janes	Frank L. Packard
Arthur Schnitzler	Donald Keyhoe	Frank V. Webster
Atticus	Dorothy Kilner	Frederic Stewart Isham
B.H. Baden-Powell	Dougan Clark	Frederick Trevor Hill
B. M. Bower	Douglas Fairbanks	Frederick Winslow Taylor
B. C. Chatterjee	E. Nesbit	Friedrich Kerst
Baroness Emmuska Orczy	E.P.Roe	Friedrich Nietzsche
Baroness Orczy	E. Phillips Oppenheim	Fyodor Dostoyevsky
Basil King	Earl Barnes	G.A. Henty
Bayard Taylor	Edgar Rice Burroughs	G.K. Chesterton
Ben Macomber	Edith Van Dyne	Gabrielle E. Jackson
Bertha Muzzy Bower	Edith Wharton	Garrett P. Serviss
Bjornstjerne Bjornson	Edward Everett Hale	Gaston Leroux
Booth Tarkington	Edward J. O'Biren	George A. Warren
Boyd Cable	Edward S. Ellis	George Ade
Bram Stoker	Edwin L. Arnold	Geroge Bernard Shaw
C. Collodi	Eleanor Atkins	George Durston
C. E. Orr	Eliot Gregory	George Ebers

George Eliot
George Gissing
George MacDonald
George Meredith
George Orwell
George Sylvester Viereck
George Tucker
George W. Cable
George Wharton James
Gertrude Atherton
Gordon Casserly
Grace E. King
Grace Gallatin
Grace Greenwood
Grant Allen
Guillermo A. Sherwell
Gulielma Zollinger
Gustav Flaubert
H. A. Cody
H. B. Irving
H.C. Bailey
H. G. Wells
H. H. Munro
H. Irving Hancock
H. Rider Haggard
H. W. C. Davis
Haldeman Julius
Hall Caine
Hamilton Wright Mabie
Hans Christian Andersen
Harold Avery
Harold McGrath
Harriet Beecher Stowe
Harry Castlemon
Harry Coghill
Harry Houidini
Hayden Carruth
Helent Hunt Jackson
Helen Nicolay
Hendrik Conscience
Hendy David Thoreau
Henri Barbusse
Henrik Ibsen
Henry Adams
Henry Ford
Henry Frost
Henry James
Henry Jones Ford
Henry Seton Merriman
Henry W Longfellow
Herbert A. Giles

Herbert Carter
Herbert N. Casson
Herman Hesse
Hildegard G. Frey
Homer
Honore De Balzac
Horace B. Day
Horace Walpole
Horatio Alger Jr.
Howard Pyle
Howard R. Garis
Hugh Lofting
Hugh Walpole
Humphry Ward
Ian Maclaren
Inez Haynes Gillmore
Irving Bacheller
Isabel Hornibrook
Israel Abrahams
Ivan Turgenev
J.G.Austin
J. Henri Fabre
J. M. Barrie
J. Macdonald Oxley
J. S. Fletcher
J. S. Knowles
J. Storer Clouston
Jack London
Jacob Abbott
James Allen
James Andrews
James Baldwin
James Branch Cabell
James DeMille
James Joyce
James Lane Allen
James Lane Allen
James Oliver Curwood
James Oppenheim
James Otis
James R. Driscoll
Jane Austen
Jane L. Stewart
Janet Aldridge
Jens Peter Jacobsen
Jerome K. Jerome
John Burroughs
John Cournos
John F. Kennedy
John Gay
John Glasworthy

John Habberton
John Joy Bell
John Kendrick Bangs
John Milton
John Philip Sousa
Jonas Lauritz Idemil Lie
Jonathan Swift
Joseph A. Altsheler
Joseph Carey
Joseph Conrad
Joseph E. Badger Jr
Joseph Hergesheimer
Joseph Jacobs
Jules Vernes
Julian Hawthrone
Julie A Lippmann
Justin Huntly McCarthy
Kakuzo Okakura
Kenneth Grahame
Kenneth McGaffey
Kate Langley Bosher
Kate Langley Bosher
Katherine Cecil Thurston
Katherine Stokes
L. A. Abbot
L. T. Meade
L. Frank Baum
Latta Griswold
Laura Dent Crane
Laura Lee Hope
Laurence Housman
Lawrence Beasley
Leo Tolstoy
Leonid Andreyev
Lewis Carroll
Lewis Sperry Chafer
Lilian Bell
Lloyd Osbourne
Louis Hughes
Louis Tracy
Louisa May Alcott
Lucy Fitch Perkins
Lucy Maud Montgomery
Luther Benson
Lydia Miller Middleton
Lyndon Orr
M. Corvus
M. H. Adams
Margaret E. Sangster
Margret Howth
Margaret Vandercook

Margret Penrose
Maria Edgeworth
Maria Thompson Daviess
Mariano Azuela
Marion Polk Angellotti
Mark Overton
Mark Twain
Mary Austin
Mary Catherine Crowley
Mary Cole
Mary Hastings Bradley
Mary Roberts Rinehart
Mary Rowlandson
M. Wollstonecraft Shelley
Maud Lindsay
Max Beerbohm
Myra Kelly
Nathaniel Hawthrone
Nicolo Machiavelli
O. F. Walton
Oscar Wilde
Owen Johnson
P.G. Wodehouse
Paul and Mabel Thorne
Paul G. Tomlinson
Paul Severing
Percy Brebner
Peter B. Kyne
Plato
R. Derby Holmes
R. L. Stevenson
R. S. Ball
Rabindranath Tagore
Rahul Alvares
Ralph Bonehill
Ralph Henry Barbour
Ralph Victor
Ralph Waldo Emmerson
Rene Descartes
Rex Beach

Rex E. Beach
Richard Harding Davis
Richard Jefferies
Richard Le Gallienne
Robert Barr
Robert Frost
Robert Gordon Anderson
Robert L. Drake
Robert Lansing
Robert Lynd
Robert Michael Ballantyne
Robert W. Chambers
Rosa Nouchette Carey
Rudyard Kipling
Samuel B. Allison
Samuel Hopkins Adams
Sarah Bernhardt
Sarah C. Hallowell
Selma Lagerlof
Sherwood Anderson
Sigmund Freud
Standish O'Grady
Stanley Weyman
Stella Benson
Stella M. Francis
Stephen Crane
Stewart Edward White
Stijn Streuvels
Swami Abhedananda
Swami Parmananda
T. S. Ackland
T. S. Arthur
The Princess Der Ling
Thomas A. Janvier
Thomas A Kempis
Thomas Anderton
Thomas Bailey Aldrich
Thomas Bulfinch
Thomas De Quincey
Thomas Dixon

Thomas H. Huxley
Thomas Hardy
Thomas More
Thornton W. Burgess
U. S. Grant
Valentine Williams
Various Authors
Vaughan Kester
Victor Appleton
Victoria Cross
Virginia Woolf
Wadsworth Camp
Walter Camp
Walter Scott
Washington Irving
Wilbur Lawton
Wilkie Collins
Willa Cather
Willard F. Baker
William Dean Howells
William le Queux
W. Makepeace Thackeray
William W. Walter
William Shakespeare
Winston Churchill
Yei Theodora Ozaki
Yogi Ramacharaka
Young E. Allison
Zane Grey

www.ingramcontent.com/pod-product-compliance
Lightning Source LLC
Chambersburg PA
CBHW020504100426
42813CB00030B/3113/J